A
STRANGE
LITTLE PLACE

© Kelsey Goodwin

About the Author

Brennan Storr is a researcher and storyteller who has written articles for several publications, including the *Diversity Reporter* and the *Revelstoke Current*. As a former Atheist turned believer, he likes to say if there is such a thing as a reluctant paranormal investigator, he is that.

Brennan lives and works in Victoria, British Columbia, Canada.

BRENNAN STORR

A
STRANGE
LITTLE PLACE

The Hauntings & Unexplained
Events of One Small Town

Llewellyn Publications
Woodbury, Minnesota

FIRST EDITION
Second Printing, 2017

Cover art: iStockphoto.com/6566560/©filo
iStockphoto.com/13348235/©Patrick Ellis
iStockphoto.com/21120520/©LuVo
Shutterstock/132786641/©kak2s
Cover design: Kevin R. Brown
Editing: Rosemary Wallner
Interior photographs: © Mike Kozek, www.mikekozek.com

Llewellyn Publications is a registered trademark of Llewellyn Worldwide Ltd.

Library of Congress Cataloging-in-Publication Data

Names: Storr, Brennan, author.
Title: A strange little place : the hauntings and unexplained events of one
    small town / Brennan Storr.
Description: Woodbury, Minnesota : Llewellyn Publications, [2016]
Identifiers: LCCN 2016012769 (print) | LCCN 2016018168 (ebook) | ISBN
    9780738748238 | ISBN 9780738749648 ()
Subjects: LCSH: Haunted places—British Columbia—Revelstoke.
Classification: LCC BF1472.C2 S76 2016 (print) | LCC BF1472.C2 (ebook) | DDC
    133.109711/68—dc23
LC record available at https://lccn.loc.gov/2016012769

Llewellyn Publications
A Division of Llewellyn Worldwide Ltd.
2143 Wooddale Drive
Woodbury, MN 55125-2989
www.llewellyn.com

Printed in the United States of America

Contents

Acknowledgments

First, my wife, Nicky Storr, who supported and encouraged me through the three years it took to research, write, and edit this project. She also put up with my telling countless ghost stories in any and every social setting we happened to find ourselves in.

My mother, Cathy Storr; sister Sara; and aunt Susan Holdener, for bringing me material and helping me vet potential witnesses to weed out the crazies. And there were crazies. Oh were there crazies.

Mike Kozek, for his stellar pictures and the hours of great conversation.

Joey Smith, for reading my many drafts and offering her insight on how to make them better. Also for listening to hours of my rambling on the subject of Revelstoke's paranormal history during our drives around Victoria.

Tom Redhead, for the science and introducing me to Miles Davis. Without *Sketches of Spain* this damned thing wouldn't have gotten finished.

Bob McIntosh, for editing the completed draft manuscripts and helping make me look less grammatically challenged than I truly am.

Mike Cyronek, for his help in bringing me people and their stories. Also for that late-night trespassing session in 2012, which helped give me the idea to write this book in the first place. Most importantly, for not getting all weird when I started dropping words like "Shadow People" and "ultraterrestrials" in conversation.

Susan Kincaid, for being so helpful in gathering material and making connections it actually defies description. Seriously —I doubt this book would have been written without her.

Dan Eastabrook, for listening and asking the hard questions.

Sami Lingren, for the photographs and all the legwork, the latter of which I know can be a real pain in the ass.

My employers Doug Williams and Melissa Hadley, who allowed me the time off to go roaming hither and yon asking strange questions, and who have never once commented on the growing library of paranormal books in my office.

And to the following people, for providing support and background information:

Gloria Abbott, Max Amsler, Olympe and Joan Astra, Stephanie Ballandine, Frank Bradford, Beckie Campbell, Spence Carefoot, Squeak Carlson, Ray Cretelli, Professor James Dickson, Cathy English, Michelle Flynn, Annette Fuoco, Gordie Gattafoni, Bert Van Goor, Bruce Haggerstone, Annie Hewitt, Evelyn Howery, Frieda Howery, Aaron Irmen, Debbie Jackson, Barb Johnson, Kevin Keates, Shelley Klassen, Candace and Carol Komishin, Andrew Mack, Diane Mahoney, Joe Martini, Diane Mayberry, Mark McKay, John Morrison, Roger Morrison, Clare Mount, Larry Nelles, Shawn Newsome, Larry Pawlitsky, Tracy Schiller, Carol Thompson, Dan Threatful, Justine Winser, Stella Weeks, Alan Young.

Apologies in advance to anyone I missed.

Foreword

In my work as a paranormal podcaster, my main stock in trade is that of the ghost story. Over the last six years on my *Campfire* podcast, I have talked to hundreds of experiencers about their strange stories of the supernatural. I take the broad view and speak with people from around the globe; however, sometimes it is even more intriguing to look specifically at one community, one town, to examine its soul and its stories.

This is exactly what Brennan Storr has done in *A Strange Little Place: The Hauntings and Unexplained Events of One Small Town*. Brennan takes us to the picturesque community of Revelstoke. With a current population of about 7,200 people, you might think there wouldn't be a lot to tell, but you'd most definitely be wrong.

In the 1880s, Revelstoke began as a transportation and supply center for the mining industry, so you can only imagine the hearty souls who inhabited this beautiful but wild spot in western Canada. From Brennan's work contained in these pages, it appears that some of them liked it so much that they decided to take up *permanent* residence!

Whether they are tales from Revelstoke Hospital, "The House on the Bank," or any of the generous number of haunted locales that Brennan shares, be prepared to be chilled from the honest retelling of terrifying tales.

The oral tradition is important but it has one flaw. If only spoken but in no way codified, stories first lose their authenticity and eventually they just cease to exist. The last storyteller moves onto the Great Beyond and the stories are lost forever.

This is why I applaud Brennan Storr and the people of Revelstoke. With the publication of this book, they have ensured these true stories are shared with generations to come. Plus, they are just damned good ghost stories. I am very honored to play even a small role in its birth.

Step One: Buy this book.

Step Two: Snuggle up with a blanket (optionally with a significant other to provide some comfort).

Step Three: Read on. If you love a good ghost story, I know you'll enjoy *A Strange Little Place: The Hauntings and Unexplained Events of One Small Town.*

Stay spooky,

—Jim Harold
July 2015
JimHarold.com

Introduction

I'll be straight—if you think ghosts, UFOs, Sasquatch, and the like are all nonsense of the highest order, I have no intention of trying to convince you otherwise. Before starting this book in April 2012, I was in the same boat, and it was only after three years of reading, interviews, and personal experience that I changed my mind; even now I retain a healthy skepticism. Without all that, there's no way in hell a few hundred pages of anything would have changed my mind, and so I wouldn't dream of trying to change yours.

Hell, this wasn't even originally intended to be a book—the plan was to record the ghost stories my mother used to tell about the house where she grew up as a sort of family history project. Once we sat down to record, however, it turned out that my mother didn't recall many of the stories from her childhood (the few she did are included in Chapter 15, "The Rota House") but she put me in touch with a friend of hers who had stories from elsewhere in Revelstoke, our hometown. Those stories put the hook in me, and I decided to see if there were enough of them around town to fill an entire book. Three years later, I've lost a couple of friends who thought I'd gone off the reservation when

I started talking about this stuff, was touched by Shadow People, was exorcised, and uncovered enough paranormal history to make up the volume you hold in your hands.

Revelstoke, British Columbia,
is a picturesque town nestled in the mountains.

Harsh Conditions to a Thriving City

At first blush you'd be forgiven for thinking there isn't much going on in Revelstoke aside from sweeping mountain vistas—the population hasn't risen above 7,500 in a decade, and each compass direction leading out of town either dead-ends in a dam (north), a lake (south), or passes through treacherous highway, which, depending on the season, can be closed for days by mudslide or avalanche (east, west). In fact, the road leading out of town to the east has been declared the most dangerous in the province of British Columbia, with thirty-eight fatal crashes in the last ten years. One of the reasons I moved away was the appeal of living somewhere where traveling in the winter doesn't necessarily mean taking your life in your hands.

Travel in the Revelstoke area has been dangerous for a long time. North of town, now lost beneath the Columbia River reservoir, is a stretch of water once infamously known as the "Dalles des Morts," or "Death Rapids," which earned their name in 1817 when a group of French-Canadian fur traders lost their boats and provisions in the turbulent water; as the men died one by one from starvation and exposure, the survivors were forced to resort to cannibalism in order to stay alive. In the end, only one man was rescued.

In 1838 the Dalles de Morts struck again when a ferry barge was swamped while traversing the rapids; of the twenty-six people aboard, only fourteen escaped with their lives. According to records from the era, the first notification people downriver had of the disaster came in the form of the barge's empty, busted hulk drifting ashore.

What kept people coming despite all the obvious peril? Money was the first motivator—the Big Bend Gold Rush of 1866 brought people en masse to Big Bend Country (so named for the hairpin curve of the Columbia River) just north of where Revelstoke now sits, though once the boom collapsed most moved on to other mineral-rich areas nearby.

Revelstoke (then known as Farwell, so named for the surveyor who first laid out the area) came into being in 1885 when it was designated as a convenient supply point for the east and west teams working toward the completion of Canada's transcontinental railway. Farwell was essentially one street running alongside the Columbia River (mostly on what is now Front Street in the part of town known as "lower town") and, by all accounts, as rough a place as you'd expect given the remote surroundings, with bar brawls, brothels, and varied gambling establishments.

The town was eventually renamed Revelstoke in honor of British banker Edward Baring, 1st Baron Revelstoke, who was instrumental in helping to finance the completion of the railway, though the name change didn't mean the settlement had softened; in 1905, a Japanese woman named Jenny Kiohara was brutally murdered after arguing with a local businessman named Wah Chang, from whom she and her husband, Fukushima, had recently purchased a brothel. Despite overwhelming evidence that Wah Chang had murdered Jenny in order to keep possession of the brothel he had sold along with her money, no charges were ever laid.

Eventually, Revelstoke was gentrified by prosperity. As time passed, its central location on both the Columbia River and Canadian Pacific Railway allowed it to become one of the most important cities in the interior of British Columbia, with an opera house, fully equipped YMCA, and other amenities one might only expect to find in a big city. Until World War I, Revelstoke, it seemed, was on its way to great things.

When World War I broke out, Revelstoke's population was some 5,700, so when between 600 and 1,000 Revelstoke men shipped out to serve in the trenches of Europe from 1914 to 1918, and more than a hundred were killed in action, it took something intangible, but very real, from the town. Construction projects languished, development slowed, and with the arrival of the Depression at the end of the 1920s, Revelstoke's days as an up-and-coming city were over. Since then it has survived as a mill town, its fortunes more or less connected to that of the timber industry, with all the ups and downs that implies. In recent years, however, the town has seen a boom in tourism thanks, in large part, to the development of its ski hill.

Tourism with a Side of the Paranormal

The ski hill—Revelstoke Mountain Resort, with its 5,600-foot vertical drop—is without a doubt the town's most popular feature. Every year, thousands of people from around the world descend on Revelstoke and its painfully inadequate airport, looking for adventure on the slopes and providing a huge boost to the town's economy.

What none of those tourists know—what few locals know, in fact—is that Revelstoke's paranormal history is just as breathtaking as the mountain views and includes so many types of high strangeness it reads like a conspiracy theorist's checklist: hauntings, UFOs, missing time, Sasquatch; all of these and more have been reported in the town and surrounding area. Bear in mind, in Revelstoke (as in many small towns) "reported" means "seen and kept quiet about so no one thinks you're crazy." In some cases, I had to all but pry these stories out of people, most of whom asked I not use their real names—so most of what you read here has never been told outside a small group of friends, let alone been published. I lived there for the first twenty-four years of my life, and ninety-five percent of the stories presented here were new even to me.

The stories in this book, I believe, represent a fraction of the strange activity that has happened and continues to happen in Revelstoke. I say this because the people I found who had forgotten stories, or simply refused to tell them, numbered in the dozens. How many others must there be as yet undiscovered?

Why Revelstoke?

The chapters you are about to read are, for the most part, separated by location, with subheadings to indicate multiple stories from a particular spot. A handful of chapters are about particular people rather than a location, but are similarly organized. Those locations are all around the town of Revelstoke and up to thirty miles outside city limits in all directions.

The stories told here all make sense within established paranormal frameworks; that is to say, all of the activity here has, in one way or another, been reported by reputable sources in other places. I have done my best to weed out the jumped-up horror-movie nonsense some people tried to pass off as their experiences.

But why would the paranormal affect this particular corner of the world? It is a common theory among paranormal researchers that some places are permanently more "active" than others, though no one can quite agree on why. Some believe the answers lie within the bedrock of haunted locations, that certain stones record emotional energy expended by the generations of people living above it and essentially "play it back" to those sensitive enough to see. Others think there are invisible nexus points between this and other dimensions, and it is the comings and goings of interdimensional beings that make up what we call paranormal activity.

Personally, I have no idea what makes a place haunted, though in the chapters to come I make one or two guesses. But whatever *it* is, Revelstoke has it, in sometimes terrifying abundance. After reading this book, I suspect you will agree.

CHAPTER 1
Strange Occurrences
Near Court House Square

In modern times, Court House Square, located on the north end of town, is home not only to its namesake but a number of private residences and businesses lining the four streets—Second, Third, Kootenay, and Wales—which border it. It is a quiet, comfortable neighborhood that, perhaps because of its recent, almost-famous past or something much older, happens to be the most densely haunted part of Revelstoke.

As I recorded stories about Court House Square, I came to think of it as a "thin spot": a place between this and other worlds or dimensions. If such a thing can be believed to exist, then the Court House Square is one such place and a large one at that: there are anecdotal reports of haunting in almost all of the structures in the immediate area. Not to mention the square is less than 300 yards from two of the town's most supernaturally active spots—Holten House and the old Revelstoke Hospital.

It has been suggested that the courthouse in Court House Square was built on an Indian burial site and, while not impossible, there is very little in the historical record to support such a theory. That's not to say it wasn't the case: certainly, should any remains have been discovered during the building of the original structure in 1897, they would not have been treated with the reverence they would be today. Any such discovery would likely have been, at best, quietly ignored. At worst? Try not to think about it.

In discussing this theory, a friend asked: If the reason for the paranormal activity was an Indian burial ground, why had no one reported seeing Indian ghosts? The answer is, I believe, that in a time before the air around us was humming with data, people had a greater sense of connection to the natural world, allowing them to sense these "thin spots," and they buried their dead near them because they hoped it would ease the spirits' transition into the afterlife. We may never know whether Court House Square is such a place, but after reading of its many hauntings, you'll be able to draw your own conclusions.

At the north end of Revelstoke's downtown sits Court House Square's most prominent structure: a four-story, neoclassical courthouse, an unusually grand sight for a town whose population has never risen above 10,000 people. The story behind it begins in 1895 when a sudden increase in the price of silver reignited interest in British Columbia's mines, jumpstarting the province's economy.

Erected in 1897, the first Revelstoke courthouse was quickly outgrown by the blossoming town, leading to the building of a new, expanded structure—designed by Vancouver architect Thomas Hooper—from 1911 to 1913. Since then Revelstoke has managed to survive and, at times, thrive, but it never again attained the level of importance it once held. The courthouse remains intact and still in use, albeit in a reduced capacity, and its sixteen-sided copper dome and vast Doric columns—imported from the U.S. southern state of Georgia—are a bittersweet reminder of the time when the city seemed destined for great things.

Voices in the Dark

In the 100 years since the cornerstone of Revelstoke's courthouse was laid, countless thousands of people, some in tears and others in chains, have walked its marble-lined halls. Lives have changed forever in the courtroom, judge's chambers, and conference rooms, and according to former night janitors David Han, Helen Ryder, and Dana Tarver, the emotions generated there linger long after the doors have closed.

The unusual activity reported at the Revelstoke Court House is entirely of the auditory variety, occurring after the night shift janitors begin work at 8 p.m., and appears to be more residual energy than conscious haunting. In this kind of activity, strong emotions leave an imprint on a location and play themselves out over and over until their energy is expended.

On the first floor, Ryder claims, you can hear the sound of indistinct male voices talking back and forth. The same phenomenon was also reported on the second floor near the offices of the Insurance Corporation of British Columbia by Han, who claims the conversations were often followed by the sound of a closing door. Also on that floor is where Tarver has said she could regularly hear women talking by the water fountain.

The sound of chains clattering on the floor have been heard in the courtroom, and in the stairwells between floors. More than one of the group has reported hearing the sound of children crying.

The current night janitor has experienced nothing out of the ordinary in his time at the courthouse, so it may be that the energy has simply expended itself, leaving the vast halls quiet. Or perhaps the sounds continue as they have, waiting for those with the ears to hear.

The Mute Girl

Built in 1915 and once operated as a small restaurant by a retired seaman and his wife, the vinyl-sided, two-story house across from the Revelstoke Court House has been heavily renovated over the years and now serves as a single-family home. Though its current owners have experienced nothing unusual during their decade in the home, local resident Hank Stein will never forget what he saw one night in an upstairs window.

"This would have been about 1990," says Stein. "I was walking my dogs past there, and I started hearing an unpleasant humming sound." The humming increased in volume, he says, scaring his dogs so badly they broke away and hid beneath a nearby car. At first unable to determine the origin of the noise, Stein tried to ignore it and set about looking for his dogs. After a few minutes, he says, "I looked up ... and saw this girl in the window. She was glowing." He goes on to describe the girl as being anywhere between eight and twelve years old, and "solid— transparent but solid."

"I could just barely make out her mouth," Stein remembers. "I could see that she was trying to say something."

Any sound the girl in the window may have been making, however, was rendered inaudible by the hum. Stein glanced away to continue looking for his dogs, and as he did, the humming began to fade. When he turned back toward the house, the girl in the window was gone.

The Revelstoke Court House, finished in 1913.

The House on the Bank

Behind the courthouse, built into a bank overlooking the oldest part of Revelstoke—known as "lower town"—the cozy, three-bedroom Carlson House gives little outward indication that it is home to one of the city's most storied hauntings, but for the last fifty years residents and visitors alike have come forward with reports of strange activity.

A Face in the Dark

Agnes Martin remembers a night in the 1960s when she and her boyfriend, Mike, visited her friend Jane Levitt, who was babysitting at the House on the Bank. The pair arrived long after the children had been tucked into bed upstairs and were chatting with Levitt in the living room when they were startled by a loud thumping noise from overhead. Spooked, the teens crept upstairs to find one of the children had rolled out of bed; Levitt returned the wayward toddler to sleep and the three returned to the living room.

After returning downstairs, Levitt went to draw the curtains on a large window facing out over the bank and Martin remembers her freezing when she got to the window. Levitt hurriedly closed the drapes and returned to the sofa, her face white. When asked what was wrong, Levitt wouldn't say and remained silent until the children's parents returned.

It was on the drive home that she admitted to what she had seen: an elderly, bearded man wearing a top hat who stared intently back at her from the other side of the glass—a side where there was no ground on which to stand.

Later, Martin was further taken aback when she described the man to her mother and she was told, "That's what he was supposed to look like." Her mother explained that "he" was the original owner of the house who became terminally ill and killed himself on the property rather than face a long, slow decline due to illness.

"Mommy, there's a man in my room!"

The Seeberg family—Anna, Jim, son Jon, and daughter Christine—moved to the House on the Bank in 1983 as renters with an eye toward eventually purchasing the home. That plan, according to Anna, didn't last.

"I don't think we were in that house much longer than a year," she says. "It just got too weird. We couldn't stay there anymore."

It began the night five-year-old Christine rushed into her parent's room, crying.

"Mommy, Mommy, Mommy," the child said, "there's a man in my room!"

Startled from sleep, Jim and Anna rushed to her room but found no one, and when a thorough search of the house revealed no intruders, they attributed their daughter's outburst to nightmares and an overactive imagination. When it happened again and again at irregular intervals over the next few months, Anna remembers telling Christine, "It's okay, honey; go back to bed; he's not really there."

Eventually, Anna says, the frequency of the "nightmares" began to increase and so did their intensity. Still, the family believed it was Christine adjusting to her new surroundings until three events, one each in spring, summer, and fall, made the Seebergs realize they weren't the only ones living in their home.

An Unseen Force

One evening in the spring of 1983, Jim Seeberg had the family's first physical encounter with the house's spirits. Earlier in the day, Jim had been at Revelstoke's Queen Victoria Hospital having his wisdom teeth removed and had chosen not to take his prescribed pain medication before going to bed. Sometime after midnight, the throbbing in his mouth reached fever pitch and Jim decided to take his pills, which were in the downstairs bathroom. At the staircase, he had descended the first few steps when a hard push from an unseen force sent him the rest of the way down.

Lying in a dazed heap on the ground, Jim tried to figure out what had happened: there was no one around to push him, so he theorized he had missed a step on the way down, gravity taking care of the rest.

"I remember thinking," he says, "that maybe I lost too much blood when they took my teeth out that afternoon."

Rising partway to his feet, Jim was immediately slammed back to the ground. Frantically, he looked for an attacker but, just as in his search for Christine's phantom, saw nothing but the darkness, broken in places by shafts of streetlight through the windows.

Since he no longer felt safe trying to stand, Jim resolved to drag himself along the floor into the next-door sitting room. Inch by inch he made his way out of the kitchen on his elbows and belly—tensing at every noise, certain he would again be struck down—until finally he managed to climb onto the sitting room sofa. Completely drained by the experience, unable even to call for help, Jim lay there listening for signs of an intruder, hearing only passing cars and the tick of the clock. When Anna found him the next morning, he was no more able to explain what had happened to him than he had been the night before.

Though they wrote off the events of the previous night to pain and blood loss, the incident still troubled the young couple. Neither of them was inclined to believe in the supernatural, but the possibility that there was something of that nature happening in their home was beginning to take shape in their minds. When Christine's shadow man paid one final, frightening visit that fall, the Seebergs realized they could no longer stay in the House on the Bank.

"Mommy, the man is in my room again!"

Though Jim's ordeal on the stairs was hard to explain, it was the man in Christine's room who ultimately persuaded them to leave. Almost thirty years later, Christine has no recollection of the events that took place in the House on the Bank, but both Anna and Katrina, the family's former babysitter, remember them well.

Because of the spectral man's nocturnal visits, Christine never felt comfortable in her own bed. She often asked to bunk with Jon in his room on the main floor, and on the infrequent occasions when Jim and Anna went out for the night, they let her do just that. Katrina, then a teenager, remembers the night Christine called her into Jon's room because, she said, "The man is staring at us."

Earlier in the evening, the teenager had been in the main-floor living room watching television when she was overcome with the certainty that someone was on the outside of the house looking in. Jim and Anna had made sure not to mention anything about ghosts to the teen because, in Anna's words, "You don't tell babysitters that your house might be haunted because you don't get babysitters," so the girl dismissed her unease. When Christine emerged from Jon's room talking about a man looking at the children through a window, however, her discomfort returned full force.

Entering the room, she was shocked to find it almost fifteen degrees colder than the rest of the house. Jon was still fast asleep, and when she looked out the window, there was no man to be seen. Still, Christine was adamant he'd been there.

"He was right there!" she insisted, pointing to a spot just beyond the window.

Afterward, Katrina went through the house locking all the doors and sat with Christine until her parents came home. She remembers the girl saying, "I think he used to live here," but not being able to explain where the thought came from.

Finally, in the winter of 1983 Christine's phantom got too close for comfort and the family decided they had had enough. Anna remembers the night Christine ran into her parents' room crying.

"Mommy!" she said. "The man is back in my room!"

As on previous occasions, Anna told her daughter that the man wasn't real and couldn't hurt her.

"Honey," she said, "just go back to your room."

This time the frightened girl stood rooted to the spot.

"Mommy, I can't," Christine said, "he's going through my dresser."

At that, Anna sat up.

"What?"

"He opened the windows and he was on the ledge of my window and then jumped on my dresser. Now he's going through my drawers."

That was enough to send Anna racing down the hallway into her daughter's room. She didn't see a man but the window—its latch too high for the child to reach—was wide open and so were the drawers of her little bureau.

"I told her," remembers Anna, "she could stay with Mommy and Daddy tonight."

That night was the final straw, and the family began looking for a new home almost immediately.

"We told the people who owned it that we couldn't live here," says Anna. "We were hoping to buy that place ... [but] there was just no way."

A Haunted Past

Had the Seebergs known Martin Vickers, their experiences in the House on the Bank might not have come as such a surprise. Though he never lived in the house, his aunt and uncle—Ralph and Grace Carlson—owned the property from the 1930s through the 1970s, and Martin was privy to many of the encounters they had.

"For me, there wasn't a great deal that was out of the ordinary," says Vickers, who stayed in the home a number of times in the 1940s and again in the 1960s. "The creaking of the stairs was about all I ever noticed, which you could maybe—maybe—construe as very soft footfall up and down."

The experiences of his aunt and uncle, however, were much more interesting.

"I remember my aunt saying to me that the spirits came along and whopped her husband," says Vickers. "They'd do it when he'd go up the stairs—they'd whack him on the rear end."

As a matter of fact, the most common place for the Carlsons to experience their house's strange behavior was the staircase; as it turns out, Jim Seeberg's encounter wasn't as unusual as he had thought.

"My uncle—I guess he stood about six feet, three inches, a big man—was going up the stairs one night," says Vickers. "He got pushed aside [by something he couldn't see]. From that moment on, he was a believer in the spook."

Vickers's aunt, Grace, was also a target for the troublesome spirit, being "bumped" a number of times, Vickers says.

"One time," he remembers, "she was carrying a load of laundry ... when the spirit pushed her and she dropped her laundry basket. Auntie was annoyed, because in those days laundry was quite difficult to do."

The Carlson daughters support Vickers's recollection. Daughter Marlene recalls:

"We'd be sitting watching TV and we'd ask Mom and Dad who was going up and down the stairs. Mom always said it was just the stairs creaking and not to worry. So of course we bought the story."

As the children grew up, they became suspicious of their mother's explanation.

"As we got older," remembers Marlene, "we thought, who the heck is that? We had a big curtain across the bottom of the stairway to keep the draft out, and when we heard the footsteps, we would go pull the curtain aside and look."

Thinking he would solve the problem once and for all, Ralph Carlson eventually relocated the stairs from the living room.

"Dad thought moving the staircase would keep us quiet, so he tried it ... but it didn't matter," says Marlene. "We would all be watching TV, talking, or playing games at the dining room table, and we'd still hear someone go upstairs. It sounded like they were really busy working around the beds. Then you'd hear them come downstairs again."

No matter how carefully they tried creeping up on the staircase, the Carlsons never did see whatever was making the noises.

The Carlsons were witness to a number of visible apparitions in places other than the staircase, however.

"My aunt, she used to see an apparition quite often ... drifting in and out of the walls," says Vickers. "She was very matter-of-fact about it. On another occasion, [my uncle] saw something which troubled him."

The apparition that had disturbed Ralph Carlson was that of a headless man walking across his living room and through the far wall.

"Uncle didn't like that at all," says Vickers. "He only saw it the once."

Vickers also recalls a visit to his aunt and uncle in the 1960s during which they hired the babysitter, Jane Levitt. The Carlsons told him that finding a sitter could be difficult because of the house's reputation. According to Grace, "We always had trouble trying to get someone to sit with our girls." When informed of the spectral man Levitt claims to have seen, Vickers says simply, "Well, that wouldn't surprise me at all."

According to him, Ralph and Grace Carlson took all the strange events happening around their home in stride. Both were hardworking, no-nonsense people—Ralph was a long-time employee of the electrical company, Grace, a dedicated home-maker—and the haunting of the House on the Bank was just another part of life they learned to deal with. And while he never saw any evidence of the haunting himself, Martin Vickers believes the stories his aunt and uncle told him.

"If they had been people who used to talk about ghosts or things like that, it wouldn't have been believable," he says. "But they were just common, everyday people. They didn't dwell on it; it just happened ... They were never really at peace with it, but ... they dealt with it, you might say. They had no choice—that was their home."

The Black Man

The only steady presence reported in the home was the spirit the Carlsons referred to as either "the Black Man," or later as "Casper" by Marlene and Barbara, the Carlsons' daughters.

"The one they called the Black Man ... seemed to be someone who wanted to comfort, especially a child," remembers Martin Vickers. "He would just sit at the child's crib ... not doing anything, but if she was disturbed or started to cry, then he would stroke her head and she would go right back to sleep. They saw him quite frequently."

Marlene Carlson remembers the Black Man vividly:

"He had ... I call it a preacher hat—a black hat with a wide brim, a long black riding coat, and black boots on. That's where we got 'the Black Man' from," she says. "You couldn't look at him and recognize him—the hat was always down so that you couldn't see his face. There were two bedrooms upstairs, and he would lean on the doorjamb of one, always on his right arm, and put his fist on his head. His left foot would always be casually pointed up. He would just stand there and watch."

Marlene says that despite the apparition's face being obscured, her family believed the Black Man to be Grace's father, Thomas Edwards, who shot himself on the property in 1941 after a long struggle with throat cancer. Edwards was the original owner of the House on the Bank, the man whom Jane Levitt believes she saw that night in the 1960s.

"My mother said that it was very usual for her father to wear a long black riding coat and black broad-brimmed hat," remembers Marlene. "Because when he was alive, he spent most of his life as a cattle rustler in Montana. She knew when he was going back out on the range because that's how he dressed."

Edwards was never without his signature black hat, Marlene says: "Even if he had a suit on, he always had that black hat too. And that's why my mother believed so strongly that it was him."

True to Martin Vickers's assessment of how the Carlsons treated the supernatural in their home, Grace was nonchalant when she would see the specter, something Marlene says would happen "in broad daylight, after dinner, when it was dark, pretty much whenever." Marlene says Grace would greet the Black Man by saying, "Hello, Dad," and he would promptly disappear.

"There was never anything broken; he wasn't a poltergeist, he never hurt anybody, he never touched you, never screamed, yelled, talked—nothing," says Marlene. "He just watched. My sister and I grew up with him; he was practically part of the family. We started calling him Casper, like the friendly ghost."

In time, Ralph and Grace's grandchildren would see Casper too, though not growing up with him meant they were far less comfortable in his presence.

"This would be some time in the late sixties or early seventies," remembers Marlene. "I was married, had two kids, and was living in Vernon [a small city about two hours west of Revelstoke]. My kids were probably four and six, so when we would go to Revelstoke to visit my parents, I would tell them to go play upstairs in the playroom."

The second-floor playroom was the same one the Carlson girls had enjoyed as children and, according to Marlene, was kept by her parents in the same condition it had been back then.

"We had taken my kids to Revelstoke maybe three or four times, but of course, we never told them about Casper," she says. "One day, my eldest came down and said, 'We don't want to play up there anymore.' I said, 'Is it too cold? We can turn the heat up.'"

The boy looked at his mother and said, "No, we're tired of that man watching us all the time."

The elder Carlsons looked at one another.

"What do you mean you're tired of him?" Marlene asked.

"Every time we come here, we go up there and play and he watches us. We're tired of it, and we're not going up there anymore."

Ralph and Grace Carlson eventually moved from the home, but as we now know from the stories of the Seeberg family, Casper remained. If it is Edwards, one wonders if he's still there, leaning against the doorjamb, watching over the home's latest residents and dreaming of Montana's wide-open spaces.

CHAPTER 2

Ghosts of the Revelstoke Hospital

Both of Revelstoke's former hospitals have their associated ghost stories, but those of the original Revelstoke Hospital are by far the most documented. That said, none of this chapter would have been possible without the help of one former resident who was happy to sit for hours of interview and conversation on the subject of the paranormal. Their family is not inclined to belief and so they have requested to remain anonymous, but they know who they are. The current residents were kind enough to let me view the building's interior, and although it was under renovation at the time, it still retains an enormous amount of character and charm.

The final story, in which a spirit helps save the home from accidental destruction, is one of my favorites because, much like Chapter 4, "That Dog in the Window," it represents a narrative rarely seen in ghost stories: ghosts with interests other than scaring the daylights out of people.

y hope that the respectful treatment of the stories
̶c̶i̶o̶w will encourage other past residents to come forward
with their experiences.

Standing at the top of the Douglas Street Hill at the entrance to "lower town," Revelstoke Hospital was the community's first, opened by Drs. W. B. McKechnie and F. W. Jeffs in 1897. Though small by modern standards—it could only accommodate seven patients at any one time—Revelstoke Hospital served the community well until 1901, when funding became available to start work on the larger Queen Victoria Cottage Hospital.

The decommissioned hospital was then purchased and converted into a private home by James Pyle Sutherland, a native of Windsor, Nova Scotia, who had come west in 1885. Sutherland had done well for himself in careers from bookkeeping to butchery since leaving home as a nineteen-year-old, and by 1901 was partnered with Charles Holten and Thomas Downs in the local Enterprise Brewery. Sutherland was also a married man, having wed twenty-eight-year-old Kathleen McLean in September 1900 at Holten's striking First Street home "Holten House."

The Sutherlands' first daughter, Agnes, was still an infant when the family moved into their new home, but by 1905 she was the eldest of three daughters, and in the years that followed the girls made a game of frightening one another in the long, dark halls of the old hospital.

"We enjoyed scaring ourselves and our playmates with stories of what might be lurking in the depths of the cellar or the attic cubbyholes," Agnes once wrote. "In the winter, when a blizzard wind whipped round the place, the attic floorboards creaked with what we were sure were the footsteps of some long-departed patient trying to find his way to the top of the stairway and ... out through the unopened front door into the winter storm."

As the years passed, the Sutherland girls married and moved away—Kathy and Doris to the United States, Agnes to Cranbrook, British Columbia—so when Kathleen succumbed to complications of influenza in 1922 and James to heart failure in 1956, the Revelstoke Hospital was left empty, save for its ghosts—those the girls had imagined and those much more real.

"We'd only been in the house a month"

Mary Whittaker says her family's introduction to the ghosts of Revelstoke Hospital came shortly after moving in.

"We'd only been in the house a month," she remembers. "We'd smell bread being baked, and bacon and eggs, but no one was cooking and the smell was too strong to be coming from a neighbor's house."

Shortly thereafter, the Whittakers began to feel as though they were being watched; the family would often hear phantom footsteps throughout the house and indistinct whispering in empty rooms.

"There was nobody in the house ... but you'd hear somebody call you," remembers Whittaker. "That didn't happen too often but it happened."

She recalls how the family's Labrador retriever would often "stare at one particular spot ... growling and inching away."

Whittaker also remembers an "uneasy feeling" near their washing machine and dryer, in the far corner of the house's expansive basement.

"I hated—just hated—to go do the laundry," she says. "Not that it's anyone's favorite job."

Eventually the feeling became so strong that she sought the help of a psychic, who explained that what she was feeling was the presence of a girl who had been abused in the basement years before. The two spoke to the entity, telling her she was free—no longer bound to the basement and the terrible memories it held.

"Since then," says Whittaker. "I've never had that feeling again."

"She would see a man standing there"

The small, rose-wallpapered room belonging to Mary's daughter, Dina, turned out to be the most spiritually active room in the house, and the girl was first among the Whittakers to see a presence.

"Dina would have been just over three years old, and around Christmastime she got really sick," remembers Whittaker. "She had the mumps, but we didn't know, at least not at first. Every time she looked over at this one spot in her room, she would see a man standing there ... it was scaring her."

On occasion, Dina would also see a young girl not much older than herself silently watching her from the side of the bed. At first, the family attributed these visions to Dina's fever, but when they persisted afterward—long into the girl's teen years, when one of them would save her life—they realized what she was seeing was very real.

Visible Spirits

While Dina may have been the first among the Whittakers to see spirits in the family home, she was certainly not the last; both her mother and her younger brother, Michael, would come to have their own encounters with the ghosts of Revelstoke Hospital.

It was around 2:30 in the morning when Mary Whittaker saw her first apparition. Stepping out of the second-floor bathroom, she came face-to-face with an elderly gentleman standing at the top of the stairs. He was wearing a white undershirt, red suspenders, and old-fashioned dress trousers.

"He looked as surprised to see me as I was to see him," she says. "I didn't really know what to do, so I kept walking back to my room. When I finally poked my head out again he was gone."

No footsteps marked the elderly man's departure and no doors were heard to open and close. He had simply disappeared.

Whittaker says Michael—who, along with his sister, declined to be interviewed for this book—no longer remembers the creatures he would see outside his room on the second-floor landing.

"When he was quite little, he used to see what he called Purple People," Whittaker says. "They were shadows of people in the hallway. He mentioned that a few times."

While it's possible Michael was seeing Shadow People, featureless paranormal entities often seemingly bound to a single location, Whittaker claims he never experienced the strong feelings of dread most often provoked by those encounters. Certainly, my visit to the home was free of any such heaviness.

"They loved the house just as much as we did"

Although the spirits in Revelstoke Hospital were never threatening, they could be bothersome at times. During renovations, the Whittakers found that not only did the house become more active but also the ghosts started to manifest a mischievous sense of humor.

"Things would go missing and turn up in different places," says Whittaker. "It seemed to be a practical joke…mainly on my husband, who isn't a believer in this kind of stuff. If he was working on something, he'd leave a room and come back to find his tools missing."

So, when Dina—then thirteen years old—came downstairs one night to complain about an irksome spirit in her room, the Whittakers believed it was the house playing another prank. They quickly learned the situation couldn't have been more serious.

As Whittaker tells it, Dina came downstairs after having been in bed barely an hour.

"Mom," she said, "he's at it again. He keeps pushing blankets in my face."

Mary went upstairs to see what—if anything—could be done, and while there was no ghost or moving blankets, there was a peculiar, acrid smell to the air.

"I called my husband up and we went into the third-floor attic," she remembers. "The chimney was on fire!"

Mary's husband immediately shut down the furnace and summoned the fire department, which arrived in time to extinguish what was rapidly becoming a serious blaze. According to investigators, the chimney had ignited and burned from the top down with no apparent warning; only the family knew how the fire had really been discovered.

Dina went on to tell her parents afterward that the longer she had ignored the spirit's attempts at getting her attention, the more frantic he had become. As it turns out, this was with good reason; a look at damage left by the fire shows it was extinguished just short of a thin aluminum vent cover separating the teen's room from the chimney. Had the fire been left unchecked for much longer, the entire wall behind Dina's bed could have ignited. From there it would have consumed the aging house in short order.

After the incident, Whittaker remembers the family, her husband included, agreeing that the spirits were welcome to stay as long as they wanted.

"At that time, we were trying to think of a way to get rid of them," she says. "Afterward we decided that they could stay. I guess they loved the house just as much as we did."

Current residents of the former Revelstoke Hospital have yet to experience any paranormal phenomena. But given that the home is but a stone's throw from the heavily haunted Court House Square area where, on still nights, a strong presence can still be felt bearing down on those equipped to feel it, this quiet is unlikely to last.

CHAPTER 3

The Haunting
of Holten House

Holten House is, without a doubt, the single most storied "haunted house" in all of Revelstoke and, as with many houses considered to be haunted, much of what passes around town about Holten House is false. For instance, an often-repeated story about a child drowning in one of the second-floor bathrooms has been found to have no basis in truth, and even claims that correspond to the experiences of past residents have been wildly exaggerated. Make no mistake, I believe Holten House is haunted, but in the subtle way of real life rather than the amped-up menace of a horror film.

Regardless of what you believe, Holten House is still one of the most original and lovely homes in Revelstoke—as of this writing it is operating as the Mustang Bed & Breakfast and I encourage you to visit. The restoration work done over the last twenty years is truly breathtaking. I owe a big thank you to Rob and Nick from Mustang for being so cooperative about Holten House's inclusion here.

Thanks to David Rooney, editor of the Revelstoke Current *and former editor of the* Times-Review, *for helping me locate Gregg Chamberlain's October 2002 article on Holten House, from which the name of this chapter is borrowed. Thanks too to all the many former owners of Holten House who took the time to share their memories of what is still a very lovely place.*

Without a doubt, the best-known haunting in Revelstoke is that of Holten House. Sitting atop Farwell Hill at the north end of First Street, the dramatic two-and-a-half-story Queen Anne—with its wraparound verandah, multiple chimneys, second-floor balcony, and intricate gingerbread trim—looks every inch the Hollywood haunted house and has stories to match. From a dark presence at the top of the main staircase to the invisible, screaming man who has staked certain rooms in the home as his own, the spirits of Holten House have made themselves known to almost every one of its residents.

Chris Mack, who viewed Holten House—now a bed-and-breakfast advertised as "Not Haunted"—with an eye toward purchasing it, says it was "a gorgeous home, but the entire time I was downstairs, it felt like I was straining to see something just outside my vision."

Mack says climbing the stairs into the attic felt like "walking in a strange place on a dark night and stopping to take a breath just as the moon comes out and you see you're one step short of a cliff." He hastily left the home and afterward felt unaccountably drained for the remainder of the day. Needless to say, he did not make an offer.

Holten House is one of Revelstoke's most beautiful and historic homes.

A Storied Past

The home takes its name from Charles Holten, a wealthy, Swedish-born businessman. He made his money mining in the Kootenay region of Lardeau and had Holten House built for his new bride, Lyda, in 1897. While there is no indication of whether Holten House was haunted during the couple's life there, we do know their lives prior to meeting, which included flight from prosecution, a political scandal, and clues as to the final resting place of a famous American fugitive, were storied enough without the presence of ghosts.

Charles

Charles Holten, born Karl Hultengren, was three years old when his family emigrated from Sweden via Hull, England, aboard the British ship *Albion* in 1869. The Hultengrens first landed in New York and eventually settled in South Bend, Minnesota.

Details of his early life are scant but Karl—now referring to himself alternately as Charles Holden, Chas Holden, and Charles Holten—claims to have made his way to Canada in 1884. Because he would often give an incorrect age when filling out official documentation, it is difficult to verify Karl's claims and follow his trail west. Why Holten did this has never been determined, although it could have something to do with his parents, Christina and Jon Pettir, intentionally erring on Karl's birth date to make it appear as though he had been born in America. Certainly, Holten always declared himself a natural-born American.

We do know that in an 1887 census a man named Charles Holten, giving his age as twenty, claimed residence in Skagit County, Washington, and in July 1890 a man bearing the same name was briefly remanded to Washington State's McNeil Island Penitentiary for selling alcohol to the First Nations population. The official charge as recorded by the court registrar was "liquor to Indians"; at the time, U.S. law forbade the selling of liquor on tribal land, and in many places still does.

On August 4, 1890, Charles Holden arrived in Revelstoke with Thomas Downs, Peter Walker, and Lochrie McDonald, the group intent on prospecting for gold. After purchasing supplies in town, the foursome made their way downriver to the Lardeau region near Trout Lake to begin their search. The mining claim eventually staked by the group would become the Silver Cup Mine, one of the richest and most productive in the area. Holden and his partners would sell the mine in 1895, returning to Revelstoke wealthy men; two years later, Charles Holten—Swedish immigrant, former laborer, and mineral prospector—was the respected local landowner Revelstoke residents know today. It was then he married Eliza "Lyda" Edwards and built Holten House in her honor.

The lounge of Holten House
is a lovely place for its B&B patrons to visit.

Lyda

The path of Eliza Edwards, or Lyda, as she was known, to Revelstoke was as winding as that of her new husband. Born Eliza Victoria Silcott in Youngsville, Ohio, Lyda would have only been a year old when her father, Craven Silcott, a Democrat, lost the 1879 race for Adams County auditor in what would become a legendarily bitter contest. In 1889, the second time her father made headlines, Lyda would have been eleven—old enough to understand that her life and that of her family had changed forever.

One of Craven Silcott's greatest supporters during the 1879 election (the results of which were famously bought and paid for by the Republican party with "two-dollar bills," according to a 1911 issue of *Cosmopolitan* magazine) was a Democratic congressman named John P. Leedom. The two men became unlikely friends—Silcott the small-town merchant, Leedom the Washington, D.C., insider. When Leedom's term in Congress ended and he was named Sergeant-at-Arms of the House, he persuaded Silcott to join him in the capital as his cashier and Chief Accountant.

In Washington, Silcott was quickly caught up in the fast-paced and often sordid life of a government man, and he soon became a regular at the horse track with his well-to-do contemporaries. Somewhere along the way, he picked up a mistress, a Quebecois woman named Louise Thibault, and his new hobbies—the ponies more than the filly, admittedly—left him with substantial debt. So on November 30, 1899, Craven Edward Silcott defalcated some $75,000 from the House and fled Washington, leaving behind his now-penniless family—wife Mary, daughter Lyda, sons Jim and Eddie, and poor John Leedom, his closest friend and the man who had appointed him in the first place. The breach of trust left Leedom disgraced and made him a pariah in Washington.

Rumors ran wild. Some said that Silcott had been led astray by his French-Canadian paramour and was holed up in a Montreal boarding house; others said he had escaped into Mexico.

The truth came out in January 1890 when a reporter from the *New York Herald* managed to locate Silcott at the home of Louise Thibault's parents in Terrebonne, Quebec.

Silcott admitted that the horses had been his downfall. "It was to keep-up and be hale-fellow well-met with these same members of Congress who now are running me down that I first went to the races," he said. "My curse on the races! I wish to God I had never gone near them."

Of Louise Thibault, he said, "There is another thing I want stated, and that is that Miss Thibault, of whom such hideous falsehoods are told, had nothing to do with my fall. Had I always taken her advice, I would be in a different position today."

Before ending the conversation, Silcott told the reporter, "The day will come when I will not appear as black as I am now painted." That day never came, and that interview was the last appearance in the public record of Craven Edward Silcott. As far as the newspapers of the day were concerned, the man had simply vanished.

The following year saw the entire Silcott family relocate to New Westminster, British Columbia, where, according to an 1891 census, they were lodging with a hotel keeper named Charles Edwards—allegedly an Australian former sea captain. Despite their casual acquaintance in official documents (Mary listed herself as "married" but gave her relationship to Edwards as "lodger"), the Silcott family had taken Edwards's surname and when they relocated to Revelstoke in 1894, Edwards joined them. According to his death certificate, signed by Dr. W. B. McKechnie, when Charles Edwards succumbed to influenza in 1897 he was fifty-eight years old—the same age as famous fugitive Craven Edward Silcott.

In November of that year, Lyda married Charles Holten and the two, their storied pasts forgotten, became the toast of Revelstoke's social scene with Holten House quickly becoming its hub. The couple would go on to have two sons, Charles Edwin and Drennan.

The Holtens are gone now—their final member, Phyllis, Drennan's wife, died in 1977—but Holten House remains, and though it has known many owners over the last thirty-five years, they all agree on one thing: they were never the only ones living there.

Whether whatever lives inside Holten House is somehow related to nearby Court House Square or comes from something buried deep in its own past, it is clear that Holten House has as many secrets as its namesake.

"I always felt as though someone was going to push me down the stairs"

Of all the experiences various guests and residents have had in Holten House, those of Frances Verlaine and Audie Van Ness are by the far the most documented. The pair occupied Holten House for a number of years, and only sold when a change in Verlaine's job forced them to relocate to southern Manitoba.

Decades later, they fondly remember the four years in which they rented the house.

"We really enjoyed living in Holten House," says Verlaine. "It's a beautiful old dwelling."

"[Owners at the time] Mitch and Dev did such a beautiful job of restoring it too," adds Van Ness. Verlaine and Van Ness moved into Holten House after Mitch and Devindra Lorre, who had purchased the home seven years earlier, moved out.

*The staircase is a gorgeous piece of woodwork,
but it has a mysterious and dark presence nearby.*

For their part, the Lorres had lived in the house for seven years more or less without incident. The only thing they deemed out of the ordinary happened one summer morning during the period they were running the house as a bed-and-breakfast.

Devindra remembers a guest who was, in her words, "really off the wall, kind of a wild person." The guest had come to her after fleeing another local inn where, according to the woman, "there [was] so much bad in the air." The woman found Holten House to her liking, and over breakfast the next morning told the Lorres, "They're very happy with you. They like what you've done to the house."

"We didn't know how to take her," remembers Devindra. "We were having breakfast on a sunny, beautiful day, and she's talking away about ... I'm assuming spirits ... and a weird thing happened."

That weird thing was a picture frame hanging above the elegant, winding main staircase chose that very moment to fall and shatter on the steps.

The Lorres were nonplussed. "I didn't know what to take out of it," says Devindra. "But it's very strange it would happen on a day with no wind, no one in the house except us talking at the table and her talking about these spirits or her feelings or whatever you want to call it."

They never shared the experience with their new tenants, so, in Verlaine's words, "We came to this thing with no prior knowledge. We had no idea about the history of the house."

And yet the two quickly fell in love with everything about the home except for the main stairs.

"Standing on top of the stairwell, there was almost an overwhelming feeling that someone wanted to push you down the stairs," remembers Verlaine. "I actually fell down the stairs three times, and I'm not a clumsy guy. It was bizarre."

Teddy Bowles, a friend of Van Ness's, reported the same feeling.

"I don't have any ghost stories," says Bowles. "[But] I always felt as though someone was going to push me down the stairs."

The same goes for Jen Blair, a Vernon real estate agent who had an eye toward purchasing the home in 2003.

"This is strange, but I viewed the house three times before I had heard it was haunted," she says. "And every time I was standing at the staircase, I would stare up at the ceiling feeling like I was being watched."

Margie Vickers, another family friend, remembers taking care of the house while the couple was out of town. "I went upstairs to turn the light off and was about to go back down but suddenly felt strongly unbalanced ... I grabbed the railing because I felt like I was going to fall."

Her young daughter, Jessica, had perhaps the most chilling encounter on the stairs. Now a teenager, Jessica no longer recalls the experience, but Margie can't forget.

"I recall her staring and talking about a not-so-nice man at the top of the stairs. She wouldn't go up there."

Despite all this, Verlaine and Van Ness were enthusiastic about their new home, Van Ness in particular.

"I'm usually afraid to be by myself at night," she says. "But funny enough, when we first moved into Holten House, I felt completely safe. There was a real protected feeling in the house."

A Territorial Presence

Six months later that sense of protection vanished when Verlaine and Van Ness put the home up for sale. A presence—possibly the specter Jessica Vickers had seen at the top of the stairs—began to make itself known to the couple, a territorial presence that both agree felt male and had no love for women.

"It felt like he really hated women," says Van Ness. "But he was okay with men." Verlaine agrees, saying he was often aware of the presence but never threatened by it.

The couple's two cats began to act strangely; where previously they had been quiet, docile pets, they now resisted coming into the house and began to hiss at thin air. The upstairs hallway in particular began to be a problem area for the animals, and

Van Ness soon realized the newly active spirit had laid claim to certain areas of the house.

"Over time," says Van Ness, "I became aware of which rooms he considered his, which rooms he considered ours, and which rooms he was okay to share."

According to the couple, the presence was completely absent on the first floor but considered both the spare room and main bathroom on the second floor "his," as was the cavernous attic; the second-floor hallway was common ground. Van Ness remembers a night when her partner was out of town and she absentmindedly wandered into the main bathroom.

"He [the presence] chased me out of the bathroom … screaming at me, and I ran into one of our rooms," she says. "I never physically saw him with my eyes, but you know how, if you close your eyes when someone is yelling, you still feel the force of their emotion? That's what it felt like."

Another former owner, Grace Park, had a similar experience one night in 2004 while staying in the master bedroom. The door to the en suite bathroom was open, as were the bathroom and bedroom doors into the hallway.

"About 11 p.m. I was lying in the semi-darkness, and all of a sudden I got this creepy feeling," says Park. "My cat sat up—he was sleeping—and he looked at the bathroom door. I felt something move into the room and then out the hallway door."

Her cat continued to watch the hallway door for a few minutes until its hackles went down and it drifted off back to sleep.

The Visible Spirits

While Verlaine and Van Ness never saw the presence themselves, there are those who have.

Markus—a chef who catered for the couple—was preparing for a dinner party when he saw a tall man in what looked like jeans and a work shirt brush past him in the kitchen. Certain the man had been Verlaine or one of the guests, Markus paid little attention to what he'd seen until later in the evening. When he began to serve the meal, Markus learned that neither guests nor hosts had left their seats the entire evening.

Margie Vickers remembers bumping into someone she thought was Markus, only to turn around and see no one there.

The only mention of a visible entity beyond the first floor comes from two little girls—one now a grown woman, the other still a teenager—who lived in the house at different times. Despite being from different families and their experiences being some twenty years apart, both describe hours spent playing in Holten House's cavernous attic—so large it once held a full-size basketball net—with an invisible friend whose appearance they no longer recall.

Though she never saw a visible apparition, Grace Park had her own issues with the attic.

"I heard lots of noises in the attic," she says. "It sounded enough like footsteps to get me to go upstairs and look around. That happened pretty well steady... but only when I was there alone."

After awhile, Verlaine and Van Ness reached what they called an "agree to disagree" place with the persistent entity in their home and continued living there until the property finally sold. The pair never returned to Revelstoke, but they have no regrets about the time they spent in Holten House.

"It was the first time I'd ever been in that situation," says Verlaine. "If there was a ghost there, he kind of got used to us."

"We lived there four years in total," adds Van Ness. "So for three and a half years, his presence was around. You know he's there; you respect his space and he respected ours."

The Brothers

It's not known how far back the haunting of Holten House stretches, but according to Marlene Carlson, who spent her formative years among ghosts in the House on the Bank, the spirits were already active in the 1950s.

"This would have been in the early 1950s," she recalls. "I was in elementary school, maybe seven or eight years old. Us kids used to love to go and visit Drennan Holten. He'd always have donuts for us."

At the time, Drennan Holten was in his mid-fifties and living in the house with his older brother Charles, or Chuck, a taciturn man of whom Carlson says the neighborhood kids were far less fond.

"Chuck…we didn't like him too much—he was just creepy," she recalls. "He had piercing eyes that would look right through you…You felt like you had nothing on when he looked at you. Drennan worked out of town with my father, and sometimes they would drink beer together at one of their houses. Chuck would never carry on a conversation…He would come to get Drennan and all he would say is, 'Come home.' He was never a sociable guy."

Drennan, on the other hand, was apparently a good-natured man who enjoyed having the kids around.

"In our house, we had a ghost we called Casper, and Drennan liked to say that Casper had come to visit him. He liked pulling our leg."

Carlson says the home was grand even then, though it was beginning to slide into dilapidation around the two men, who were both bachelors at the time.

"The furniture was so fantastic," remembers Carlson. "It was right out of *Gone with the Wind*. But [the brothers] didn't give a damn about it—they just wrecked it. It was so neat ... the Victorian furniture, the wood, the upholstery. It was gorgeous ... right out of a movie."

The house would remain in this deteriorated condition until the late 1970s, when ownership passed from the Holten family to that of the Macdonnells, who would renovate the home and raise their children there before eventually selling to the Jacksons in 1990.

Like so many others, Marlene Carlson's supernatural encounter in the Holten House centered on the stairs.

"Every time my sister, Barbara, and I went to visit, we had a donut," says Carlson. "Then we had to go up the stairs, down the hall, and down the back stairs to the kitchen because we wanted to see if we could see something."

Before climbing the stairs, Barbara would grab Marlene's hand.

"She was never chicken of anything," says Marlene. "But in Drennan's house, she was chicken. We both were—we got scared every time. She'd always make me go first, and of course, I would because I'd want to see if we'd find something, but it was always just the feeling of a presence, like the hair was going up on the back of your neck."

The Carlson sisters never did see a spirit in Holten House, but Marlene is certain it was there, hiding just ahead and out of sight.

"It was almost," she says, "like whatever it was, was expecting us to come up there."

In Dreams

If the handful of people who have come forward are any indication, the influence of Holten House extends beyond its walls; a number of Revelstoke residents describe the home as having a profound effect on their dreams.

Mike Hardy, now in his fifties, would pass Holten House as a boy every day on his way to school and still vividly recalls a childhood dream about the home.

"This would have been sometime in the early to late 1960s," says Hardy. "I dreamed there was a garage, but on the north lawn, not the south where it is now. The garage door opened ... It was full of headless bodies. Then a door opened in the side of the house and someone came out. I didn't know who ... but they were coming for me."

Linda Timms, another Revelstoke resident, had a similar series of dreams about the home. In those dreams, nameless bodies lay buried in the same location where Hardy saw them stacked. There is no indication on the historical record of anything being interred on the property.

Another woman, Hanna Grimes, describes a disturbing recurring dream in which she was trapped in Holten House.

"I dreamed this for a week straight after going inside the house and had it off and on for years," she says. "Water was running everywhere and I was trying to escape or hide but there was something terrible—I don't remember what—happening in each of the rooms and I was afraid to go in them."

She can no longer recall the part of the dream in which she escaped the house, but she remembers what happened afterward.

"When I got outside, it was nighttime," she remembers. "I ran from the house, and when I was far enough away to feel safe, I turned around. That's when I saw the attic burning."

CHAPTER 4
That Dog
in the Window

Un-creepy ghost stories are something I appreciate and Barb's story of "That Dog in the Window" definitely counts as one. It's unfortunate that the immense possibilities represented by spirits are often boiled down to scare stories, as if all life leads to the opportunity to drag chains across the floor and ruin the sleep of anyone who happens to be nearby.

This is yet another haunting in the vicinity of Court House Square. While Revelstoke is a small place and it seems like we should not be overly surprised at having so many occurrences this close together, it's not that small (geographically at least) and I feel the concentration of hauntings in this area to be truly unusual. Why it is happening, or what is implied by the presence of animal spirits in the afterlife, are deep philosophical waters into which we won't be wading here.

Not far from Court House Square, lifelong Revelstoke resident Barb Johnson had an unusual experience that suggests it's not only the spirits of people roaming the land on which Revelstoke was built.

In 2006, Johnson and her husband, who were browsing real estate opportunities, requested a showing of a red-brick heritage home a stone's throw from the House on the Bank. The home, a two-story affair on a tree-shaded corner lot, is as unassuming as all of Revelstoke's other supernatural hot spots.

On the day of their viewing, the Johnsons arrived early to the appointment and so stood waiting for the real estate agent outside the home, which they had been assured was vacant. It was as they stood there that Barb first noticed the dog, which she described as looking like Toto from *The Wizard of Oz.*

"We were looking at the house, in the big picture window at the front," she remembers. "We looked at it and I said, 'What a sweet little dog!' He was wagging his tail and looking right at us."

When the real estate agent arrived, Barb asked him why, if there was no one living in the home, a dog had been left behind. The real estate agent seemed skeptical of the Johnsons' claims and assured them the home was completely vacant, with no pets left behind. Certainly, on viewing the home, Barb and her husband discovered it to be completely empty and notably lacking in dogs.

"I looked at the corner by the front window where the little dog would have been," says Johnson. "There was no way—because there was no furniture in that house and that window was a good two-and-a-half feet up. There was no way that dog could have been in the window."

Though the rest of the viewing was uneventful, the Johnsons elected not to purchase the red-brick home. Some time later, Johnson told the story to a woman, whom we will call Sandra, who had grown up in the house. Johnson discovered Sandra had once owned a small black dog that spent many a day resting comfortably in the house's large picture window.

"She told that he used to look out the window all the time!" remembers Johnson. "I guess he was quite young and was hit by a car in the street outside their house, so they buried him under the pine tree in their backyard."

Johnson asked Sandra if she had any photographs of her childhood pet so she could see whether it resembled the animal she had seen.

"It took a couple months, but she finally tracked down a picture. It was him!"

CHAPTER 5

Footsteps at the Old Drive-In

This story was one of the first I uncovered while research-
ing this book, and it was difficult to find supporting in-
formation. But the experience itself conforms to standard
paranormal tropes and the Revelstoke A&W is not far from
the extraordinarily haunted Court House Square, so I am
inclined to believe.

The first A&W restaurant was built in Portage, Manitoba, in 1956, and their take on McDonald's-style fast food quickly found an audience. Before long, drive-in burger joints popped up all over Canada and, in 1965, the by-then national chain made its way to Revelstoke. The look of the restaurant has changed over the years—as North America's car culture changed, drive-ins passed out of vogue and A&Ws across the continent were remodeled into sit-down restaurants with drive-through components—but Revelstoke's A&W still stands where it always has, next to the Trans-Canada Highway on the far north side of town.

Considerably larger than it was in 1965, the red-and-yellow restaurant is decorated with drive-in paraphernalia as a tribute to what many consider its glory days, and, according to some staff members who have worked the night shift, that's not all that remains from times past.

Current members of the late shift don't put much stock in the idea of a resident spirit. Said one employee, "We treat it as kind of a joke. I don't think anyone working here actually believes it." A supervisor who has been with the restaurant for almost twenty years echoed that sentiment:

"If it's happening, it's not happening to me and no one has ever said anything about it."

Jim Terrio, who worked in the kitchen at A&W during the 1990s, has plenty to say about it now, though at the time he had no idea the restaurant was haunted. His only clue that something was amiss was a particular quirk of his supervisor, one that only manifested at the end of the night.

"Every time she closed, she would have someone from the kitchen staff stay there with her—just sit and wait for her," he remembers. "I thought it was odd, but soon after I became a supervisor and had to do the closings myself."

It was around this time Terrio began to notice something unusual taking place around him after hours in the darkened eatery. After the other employees had gone home, he would pour himself a soda before walking the floor of the restaurant to make sure everything was properly cleaned and put away, then head to the office in the rear of the building.

"If I left my drink on, say, the front counter or in the kitchen, when I came back it would be moved. I kid you not," he remembers. "If I left it on the counter, I could find it anywhere—half the time I'd find it on the stove in the kitchen. Nobody else was in the building."

From time to time, other small articles would disappear from one place only to reappear in another, but interestingly, Terrio says, money was never touched.

"I'd leave my stuff on the counter and come back to find it on the floor, or moved against the wall or in the office. Never any damage—there was never anything malicious. Things would just...move."

On nights when he would descend to the restaurant's basement storeroom, Terrio was certain he could hear the mischievous presence above him:

"I'd go to the basement to do inventory at night...and there would be somebody running back and forth upstairs. It wasn't like a heavy 200- to 300-pound guy...just somebody small and light. Thing was, they'd only run as far as the front counter, which was as far as the original building extended—you know, when it was a drive-in."

No matter what he did, however, Terrio was never able to see whatever was sprinting across the restaurant.

"I'd climb up the stairs, and as long as I didn't put my foot on the top step, I'd still hear it," he recalls. "The second I set my foot down at the top, it was gone."

Though the incidents never frightened Terrio, they did pique his curiosity, and after leaving A&W he broached the subject with his former supervisor, who grudgingly admitted to experiencing the same things.

"It wasn't until I started talking to her that it made sense," he remembers. "She said that was why she used to get me to stay there with her at night. I thought—seriously? Some warning would have been nice."

CHAPTER 6

The Legends
of Mount Begbie

Though the universe is too vast to completely rule out the existence of extraterrestrial intelligence, I'm not a believer in most of the current theories bandied around by UFO-logists. So while what is being described in these stories, along with others later in the book, can be called UFOs, it is only because they are technically "unidentified flying objects"—whether you choose to believe they're being flown by little grey men or are a manifestation of some as-yet-unknown natural or spiritual phenomenon is entirely up to you. Special thanks to Professor James Dickson for his level-headed look at the "Mount Begbie Iceman" and willingness to discuss his work. Thanks, too, to my interviewees, most of whom asked not to be specifically identified.

Rising to a height of almost 9,000 feet, Mount Begbie is the tallest of the mountains encircling Revelstoke, and its glaciated triple peak has come to be one of the town's iconic images; the U.S. Library of Congress retains photographs of the mountain dating back to the turn of the twentieth century.

Named for B.C. Supreme Court Chief Justice Matthew Baillie Begbie—the famous "Hanging Judge"—Mount Begbie looms over the western side of the Columbia River and Arrow Lakes, its distinctive shape visible almost anywhere you stand in the region. Some twenty kilometers south of Revelstoke on Highway 23 is the trailhead that provides access to the mountain's summit. The trail, first axed out in the early 1950s, winds through fields of lupin, valerian, and Indian paintbrush on an eight-hour hike to the glacier's foot.

It is here on the glacier some 120 years ago that the stories surrounding Mount Begbie begin.

The Mount Begbie Iceman

For years, local researchers believed the legend of the Mount Begbie Iceman to have been wholly concocted in 1940 by local newspaper owner Arvid Lundell as a way to promote the opening of the Big Bend Highway.

"[Lundell] was putting it forth as a legend," says Cathy English, curator of the Revelstoke Museum and Archives, "because they were trying to encourage people to come to Revelstoke then."

English says: "The story was that it was—take your pick—a First Nations person, Big Bend miner, or fur trader who had tried to go up over Begbie, had gotten caught, and was frozen and buried in the glacier."

Then in 2007, a visit by Professor James Dickson, an expert in archaeobotany (the study of plants found at archaeological sites) at the University of Glasgow, Scotland, established the legend as being much older.

In his 2011 book *Ancient Ice Mummies*, Dickson explains:

Following a 2004 public lecture on Ötzi, a 5,000-year-old ice mummy recovered in the Ötztal Alps on the border between Austria and Italy, Dickson received a letter from a Rosamund Stenhouse-Stewart. It seems Dickson's mention during the lecture of Kwäday Dän Ts'ìnchi, a 250-year-old ice mummy found near the border of British Columbia and the Yukon, recalled in Mrs. Stenhouse-Stewart a story she had been told by her father, Thomas Livingston Haig, Revelstoke's magistrate from 1894 to 1897.

According to Dickson, Stenhouse-Stewart went on to say her father was "shown by an Indian fur trapper the body of a completely preserved Indian trapped within the ice … . I do not know where, but he mentioned its preservation and complete condition. I believe that he understood that the gathering thickness of the ice had begun to make the body gradually less visible."

For further information, Dickson contacted Alexander Mackie, the B.C. archaeologist who helped document and recover the remains of Kwäday Dän Ts'ìnchi. Mackie's inquiries weren't quite fruitless—he found mention, dating back to before and just after the 1890s, of a body frozen in a glacier somewhere near Revelstoke—but turned up nothing firm and certainly no first-person accounts of discovery.

Undeterred, Dickson journeyed to Revelstoke in 2007. He liaised with Cathy English at the Revelstoke Museum and Archives, who, along with her assistant Kirsten Gonzales, spent countless hours looking through official documents and newspaper clippings searching for some mention of Haig's alleged journey up the mountain.

No such mention was found. Indeed the only substantial piece of information on the legend was the aforementioned article, dated June 30, 1940, by Arvid Lundell of the *Revelstoke Review*—an article his daughter admitted he had fabricated from whole cloth.

A flight around the glacier by helicopter was then arranged, and Dickson finally came to a conclusion. Of the mountain, he says, "it makes little sense that there could ever have been a frozen body there."

In *Ancient Ice Mummies* Dickson describes most such finds as being in or near mountain passes. Finding a body on Mount Begbie was unlikely because there was no apparent reason for anyone, First Nations or otherwise, to climb the mountain.

"To ascend Mount Begbie," says Dickson, "is to go nowhere but up the mountain."

When asked if a member of the early First Nations could have made the ascent for religious reasons, Dickson admits it is possible but has no bearing on the existence of an ice mummy.

"It is possible that the local indigenous people attached spiritual significance to such a prominent, striking mountain," he says. "But that does not mean there was a frozen body ... . [It is] just an engaging tale. Nothing more."

Watch the Skies

While there may not be any frozen bodies on Mount Begbie, legends around the distinctive mountain continue to circulate. In particular, the mountain seems to be a lightning rod for stories of strange lights in the sky.

"*That is a really weird light*"

Jan Hartley was just a teenager when she saw her one and only occurrence of unusual lights in the sky. It was close to midnight on a New Year's Eve in the late 1970s and Hartley was walking away from her home on Second Street.

"I was by myself, going down to [a friend's] house to meet them outside," Hartley remembers. "And ... I saw a light go over Mount Begbie."

Hartley says the light, which originated in the south before breaking west over the mountain, had no definable shape or color.

"It was ... a bright light—wasn't moving very fast but wasn't blinking either," she says. "I just remember staring at it and saying to myself, 'That is a really weird light.' It was only a few seconds then it was gone."

"*Something caught the sun ...* "

Standing in the backyard of his daughter's home, in the 800 block of Second Street West, Carol Thompson's father, Earl, was the first of the family to see something strange in the shadow of Mount Begbie.

"It was a sunny day in the summer time, sometime in the late 1970s," remembers Carol. "I'd say it happened around noon or one o'clock, because my parents were over for lunch."

"My dad was leaning on the fence facing the river," she continues. "My husband, Ken, and I were in lawn chairs facing him. All of a sudden Dad says, 'Look at that!'"

Following Earl's gaze, the family observed, across the Columbia River below Begbie's triple peak, what appeared to be sunshine gleaming off metal.

The object was not visible in a traditional sense—the Thompson family could not see exactly what was catching the sun; only an outline of the mysterious object was visible. In fact, Thompson believes what she saw was only a portion of the thing's true size, a piece roughly ten feet in length.

"I don't think it was the whole picture," she remembers. "Just a glimpse. I can't help thinking something caught the sun that wasn't supposed to. A ten-foot-long section of something curved and going so fast... like a bullet. It went up along the river and past Mount Begbie School. It didn't make a sound. Then it disappeared."

To date, Thompson has never seen the object, or anything like it, again.

A trail of blue sparks

One winter night in 2004, Alan Grace and Christine Helm were on their way home to the house they shared on Highway 1. They both saw what they described as "a trail of blue sparks" traveling east to west across the night sky. Grace remembers, "They were bright, neon blue, and passed over our car before disappearing behind Mount Begbie."

"It was hovering there... it was big"

Another report of unusual activity over Mount Begbie comes from Mark Ronson, a heavy-duty mechanic and amateur astronomer who knows his way around the night sky.

"In my first years [after taking up astronomy], I was out every night when it was clear. I got to know the sky, all the stars, the constellations, and all the movements," he says. "It was so neat... not many people know that's Jupiter, that's Sirius, and so on—they think it's bright lights in the sky, and I wanted to go further."

On a spring afternoon sometime in the 1990s, Ronson would see more than he imagined.

"I was walking my dog down in the industrial park ... by the motocross track. The sun was going down, and I happened to glance up right above the ridge of Mount Begbie," he remembers. "I saw an object there. I put the binoculars on it and saw it was a brown rectangular shape. It was hovering there ... it was big ... and then all of a sudden it took off and vanished in a point of light, heading west."

Unsure of what he had seen, the first thing Ronson did was to rule out conventional explanations.

"It could have been the Hubble—that's why I went home and checked," he says. "But the Hubble wasn't in the sky that day, and neither was the Spacelab."

Even if they had been present, Ronson has a hard time believing either object would be capable of moving at the speed of the one he had seen.

"That thing took off and it was gone. I saw it go from rectangular to a point of light within a second."

CHAPTER 7

The Man
in the Field

*This story has been one of my favorites ever since Turk
Wilson (not his real name) first related it to me; I'd never
heard someone describe seeing something so unusual in
such plain terms. The property and house mentioned here
are long gone—bulldozed to make way for the new highway—and Wilson had never seen a ghost before and hasn't
since, but he adamantly stands by his account.*

Sitting on the west bank of the Columbia River, the part of Revelstoke known as Big Eddy—so named for the swirling currents
of the river's Big Bend to the north—is a strange mixture of residential, industrial, and agricultural land, bisected by the two-
lane span of Highway 23.

Until the coming of the highway, built to connect Revelstoke
with the Arrow Lakes region to the south, the Big Eddy was a
bucolic patchwork of small farms, and it is from this time that
Turk Wilson remembers seeing his first and only ghost.

Now in his seventies, Wilson was a small boy when his family
rented a farmhouse in the quiet rural community. The two-story

clapboard home had a large front porch where the family would sleep on warm summer nights, and it was next door to a large pasture where they kept a variety of livestock. The Wilsons lived in the home for several years before the property was sold and they were forced to relocate, eventually settling on another parcel of land nearby. After the move, Turk would often walk past his former home on the way to school and remembers seeing the same elderly man tending to the land.

"There was this old character," says Wilson. "I don't know whether he bought it or lived there or was looking after it or something... but I remember he always had an old black hat on."

A few years later, the old man died and the Wilson family was again offered the opportunity to rent the property. Not long after moving back, Wilson remembers how one of their cows somehow kept managing to get from their fenced pasture into the family's yard, where it would make a fantastic mess.

"We had this chain and a gate to keep her out, and that thing used to get in quite often," he says. "The chain would be undone and we were always at a loss. I guess it never occurred to anybody maybe to put a padlock on the darned thing."

For several weeks it was the same. Every night the chain would go up; every morning it would be on the ground and the family's "stupid cow" would be lazily chewing on Mrs. Wilson's flowers.

Then one summer night, Turk rose from where he had been sleeping on the porch to see, in the dusk, a man unhooking the chain from the pasture fence.

"It was almost daybreak, maybe 3 a.m., and I woke up because my two dogs—big collies—were growling," he remembers. "I turned to look at the gate, which was maybe half a block away, and could see someone standing there moving the chain. All I could see was the figure—and the black hat. Well, you know, I wasn't too anxious to get out there."

The Big Eddy Bridge spans the Columbia River.
Farms used to populate this area before the bridge was built.

After a few moments, Wilson gathered his nerve and stepped off the porch, only to see the figure disappear in the gathering light. When he reached the pasture fence, the cows were nowhere to be seen and the chain was on the ground.

Whatever the reason for the apparition, its appearance that morning was to be the last time it was seen by the Wilson family or anyone else.

"I never saw it again," says Wilson. "And we never had any more trouble with the chain, for that matter."

CHAPTER 8

The Graveyard
Next Door

Word of this story first came to me through a close friend who was always the very definition of skeptic. He was a friend of the Gates (not their real name) family and is mentioned below as the person who heard disembodied voices whispering in his ear. Though he retains a healthy skepticism, that encounter permanently changed his perspective on the subject of the paranormal. As for the house itself, the young family now living there has yet to experience anything out of the ordinary.

Given their proximity to the Revelstoke cemetery on Highway 23 north of town, there have always been rumors that burial sites were disturbed in order to make way for the Thunderbird homes. Some say a number of graves were disinterred and relocated elsewhere; others claim they were built over and remain below the homes. Official records refute these rumors but nonetheless, people in Revelstoke have whispered stories about hauntings in the Thunderbird development since its completion in 1977.

For the women of the Gates family—Maya, Emily, and mother April—the haunting in their home on Corbin Place was no mere story. From strange sounds in the night to three-year-old Maya's insistence that a man in black was sharing the family's home, the events that took place during their time in the Thunderbirds still trouble the Gates women today.

"There were voices…
but there was nothing there"

The fact that their new home bordered the graveyard, with headstones mere feet from their back fence, didn't bother April Gates or her husband; in fact, the two found the location peaceful. It was a spacious, two-story home with room for themselves; April's teenage daughter, Emily; and a new arrival that the couple was eagerly planning for. After moving in, however, April's feelings toward the home began to change.

"The air," she says, "it was always unsettling. You were always on your last nerve."

It was not long afterward that she began having what she described as "horrible nightmares" about the home. Still, the new family worked hard at making the house their own and before long had settled into a comfortable routine. This is about the time the spirits in the home made themselves known to Emily, then a teenager.

Emily remembers coming home to Corbin Place late at night on a number of occasions and hearing what sounded like electronic interference.

"It was … like somebody was listening to a TV or a radio," says Emily. "There were voices … interference like white noise … but there was nothing there."

Sometimes on nights when the radio static could be heard, Emily would also see flashes around corners and across doorways, as though someone was walking quickly past.

To visitors, the Revelstoke cemetery is a peaceful place; but some who have lived next to it feel very differently.

"I'd be brushing my teeth and someone would walk by the bathroom door," Emily remembers.

When the phenomenon first began, the girl believed her mother was up later than usual and so would call out a greeting.

"I'd say, 'Hey Mom!' but when I went out looking for her ... she wasn't there." For her part, April has said she was not the one walking past her daughter in the night.

It wasn't long before the activity at Corbin Place began to manifest itself to people outside the family too. Emily recalls the day she and April were watching television with a friend who suddenly looked toward them and asked, "Who said that?"

"We looked at him and asked what he was talking about," said April. "His face went white, and he said that someone had whispered in his ear."

"He's looking at me ... he looks really mad"

Maya was born a little over a year after the Gateses moved into the house on Corbin Place, and her birth marked an uptick in the home's paranormal activity. It began with the infant's electric baby swing, which, several times, both April and Emily saw turn itself on and start to rock.

"It would stop dead, then it would start again," remembers April.

When she was old enough to talk, Maya began to tell her parents about the strange people she was seeing around the home. First it was a young girl, her blond hair in pigtails, who would appear from nowhere and sit staring at her.

"She would be so matter-of-fact about it," says April. "I'd say, 'Maybe you were having a bad dream,' and she would always say, 'No, Mom!'"

Soon the girl was joined by another, more sinister figure—a man dressed all in black, his face covered. Maya would sometimes see what she called "the dark man" walking in the upstairs hallway near the bedrooms or downstairs in the dining room, and April remembers her daughter running to her in fear on a number of occasions.

"Mom, he's sitting there," the girl would say, gesturing to where she had been playing underneath the dining room table. "He's looking at me ... he looks really mad."

The most dramatic incident happened when Maya was four, toward the end of the Gates family's time in the house on Corbin Place. One evening after dinner, the child was sitting at the dinner table watching Emily and April put away the dishes. The last piece to go into the cupboard was a drinking glass, and as April walked away to hang up her dishtowel, the cup exploded with a bang, sending glass everywhere.

"It didn't just break; it exploded into shards that you could barely even see," says April. "It shot across the entire kitchen. We had shards of glass in our hair, on our socks, everywhere."

"Something was not right"

Though there were strange incidents all over the house, April remembers Emily's room as a hotspot for supernatural activity.

"Sometimes the room would be ice cold," she remembers. "It would bother me to walk into that room or even by it. Something was not right in there."

In addition to intermittent cold temperatures, Emily would also experience problems with the stereo in her room; while listening to music with the volume set on low, the sound level would suddenly increase to its maximum volume setting. Hoping the problem was electrical, the family sent the stereo to a repair shop, but no faults were found. The issue returned immediately after the stereo arrived back at the home.

With some hesitation, April remembers the part of Emily's room that bothered her the most—a crawl space underneath the house, entered through Emily's closet:

"There was a crawl space in that room in the closet," says April. "I'd been down to store a few things underneath there and there was a white, silty sand underneath that place and the board—you know, the floor that you cover the crawl space with—there were scratches on the underside of that board. I don't know where the hell those came from."

"There was a rage in there..."

While April claims to have heard a story about two graves being disinterred to make way for their home, one belonging to a little girl with blond pigtails, there is little hard evidence to support this claim. What does seem possible, from Emily's descriptions of flashes in the edge of her vision, Maya's description of "the dark man," and talk of anger and lingering unease, is that the house on Corbin Place had been paid visits by the entities often known as Shadow People.

For more information, see Chapter 24, "Shadow People and Gremlins."

Whatever the cause, after five years in the house on Corbin Place, the Gates family was exhausted—April split with her husband soon after they sold the property and relocated with her daughters to the Okanagan Valley, two hours southwest of Revelstoke.

"That house wasn't a peaceful place," she remembers. "There was a rage in there. It affected you. I honestly believe that's why my marriage fell apart the way it did."

Five years is, coincidentally, the amount of time the house's previous owners had lived in the home before moving on.

In the years since leaving Revelstoke, April Gates and her daughters have often looked back to their time on Corbin Place and wondered exactly what plagued the house they had come to with such optimism.

"I used to go for walks through the cemetery when I was pregnant with my daughter," she remembers. "And even afterward. I found it quite relaxing. But that house... it was dark. I felt so bad when I left there because the people moving in... they were gonna have to go through what we did."

CHAPTER 9

The Ghost
of Henry Colbeck

It's difficult to say whether the ghost spotted in the Colbeck House is truly the spirit of Henry Colbeck or an echo of his personality, a residual presence that will one day fade entirely. Certainly, the current owners of the Colbeck House have never seen any apparitions and, despite having gained quite the reputation as one of Revelstoke's haunted houses, the property has been quiet for many years.

Born in England in 1869, Henry Colbeck immigrated to Canada as a young man, marrying fellow English expatriate Ellen Page in 1894. The couple were married in the small Okanagan town of Vernon before settling in Revelstoke, where Henry worked as a marine engineer on a steamship.

As the years went on, Colbeck invested in property all over town and by 1915, when a mysterious fire claimed his ship—the S.S. *Revelstoke*—along with the small Arrow Lakes town of Comaplix, Colbeck owned much of the neighborhood north of the Highway 1 intersection, now known as Columbia Park. From this point on, Colbeck became a farmer, working his own land the way his father, George, had in England.

Henry Colbeck was a well-known and respected citizen of Revelstoke. A road off the highway bears his name.

Colbeck House—originally a modest bungalow—was built by Henry in 1908 and expanded to its current two-story incarnation in 1926 as his wealth increased.

Following Henry's and Ellen's deaths, his in 1949 and hers in 1953, ownership of their home passed into the hands of the local Masons, an organization to which Henry had belonged for many years. It was around this time that Colbeck House began to gather a reputation as one of Revelstoke's haunted houses.

The Man in the Window

Gloria Abbott, whose mother, Margaret Farness, purchased the Colbeck House sometime in the early 1960s, remembers hearing stories about its resident ghost. Abbott says Mrs. Farness would often walk into her small bedroom near the front of the house to see a spectral older man sitting in a chair.

"I don't know what that room was many years ago but it was [my mother's] bedroom then," remembers Abbott. "She said he was sitting in his chair with his seaman's cap and he was looking out the window."

Though the man never spoke, Mrs. Farness recognized Henry Colbeck from old photographs.

"She saw him a few times," says Abbott, "but she wasn't afraid of him. She said he was just there."

"There was this horrendous crash ... "

Dan and Celeste Tracy never saw Henry Colbeck during the time they lived in his house, but they heard no shortage of other stories when they moved into their new home.

"Previous owners told us when you drive by the house at night you can see lights in the attic," remembers Celeste. "Or the oven light will turn itself on when you're not in the room. We didn't experience anything like that."

In fact, for the first two years they spent in Colbeck House, the Tracys didn't experience anything at all. Then, one Sunday afternoon while Dan was working in the garage, Celeste heard a terrific noise.

"There was this horrendous crash," she remembers. "It shook the whole house. I thought maybe someone had driven off the road and hit us."

Running out the front door to find Dan, Celeste was surprised to learn he hadn't heard anything at all. A walk-around of the property showed no obvious damage—no cars half-embedded in any of the walls, for example—so the couple went inside the home to look for the source of the disturbance.

"We came back in through the front door and walked all the way around on the inside of the house to see if something had fallen. We couldn't find anything," says Celeste.

By the time they had reached the back door of the house, the pair was completely stumped. Dan was dubious at best, and Celeste was beginning to think she had imagined the whole thing. Then they saw the broken glass. Somehow, the interior pane of the back door's double-glazed window had shattered into pieces but left the exterior pane untouched.

"To this day," says Celeste, "I can't give you a logical explanation for that one."

CHAPTER 10

The Man Who Wasn't There

Many thanks to Carol Thompson for the hours-long interview she gave, which produced this and other stories. She held nothing back, and I learned a great deal from our conversations, including how the topic of the supernatural has a way of emptying nearby tables.

Though she no longer recalls the exact date, Carol Thompson remembers it was sometime in the late 1970s when she first became aware of an unexpected presence in the home she shared with her husband, Ken, and their three children.

One night, her children in bed and Ken—an engineer with the Canadian Pacific Railway—away at work, Carol had settled into her easy chair with a book and had soon fallen asleep.

"It was quite late in the night—I'd say maybe two in the morning," she remembers. "I had kicked back in my chair with a little light on to read by and I fell asleep. I woke up because something walked by me and left a breeze."

At first, Carol assumed the movement was Ken returning home from work.

"I sat up and noticed the door from the entry, which had been closed, was open, so I thought maybe my husband had come home."

Rising from her chair, Carol slowly walked toward the kitchen, where Ken would usually be found after a long shift.

"I looked into the kitchen, but everything was still dark," recalls Thompson. "So I called his name."

There was no reply.

Wondering if she had perhaps missed him in the kitchen, or if, after entering the living room, he had turned around and gone upstairs to bed, Thompson went to the window to check for her husband's car parked outside. His parking spot was empty. Carol wrote the experience off to her imagination.

"I thought it was weird, and sat back down in my chair to read."

Thompson soon fell back asleep but not for long. Around thirty minutes later she woke again.

"The same thing happened," she remembers. "Like somebody walked by me, but this time actually brushed a hand along my arm."

Again, Carol rose from her chair and again she discovered she was alone on the main floor of her house. This time, she double-checked all the locks and went upstairs to wait for Ken.

The Sleeping Man

After that night, the presence in the Thompsons' home would make itself known intermittently but never in any memorable way—at least not until the appearance of the sleeping man.

"One day, I heard something on the front porch," remembers Carol. "It was just a screened-in porch; there were no locks or anything… but still, I wasn't expecting to see a man curled up sleeping out there. He was curled up in the corner, half-sitting up against the wall."

Believing the man, who she remembers being dressed in khaki-colored trousers and a Mackinaw jacket, to be a vagrant, she decided to leave his removal to Ken.

"This fellow didn't seem to be any threat to me, but I wasn't gonna go out there and check it out," she said. "By that time, my husband wasn't working all night anymore—he'd by home by 11—so I left it."

Carol kept checking on the man, who never once moved from his spot on the floor, and when Ken arrived home, she was surprised to see him enter the house without stopping.

"Did you see the guy sleeping on the floor?" she asked.

"No, I didn't see anybody there," was his reply.

Carol immediately went to the window and, sure enough, the sleeping man was right where she had last seen him. Ken would have had to walk right past him on his way inside but had seen nothing.

"I told him that he was right there, and this time Ken saw him too," says Carol. "So he went around the corner and onto the porch. It only took a second for him to get out there, but by the time he did, the guy was gone. I never saw him again."

CHAPTER 11

The Jealous Spirit
of Main Street Cafe

The story of Main Street Cafe's transient spirit is just one of many that make a great case for hauntings not necessarily being linked to prior events in a particular location. While many paranormal researchers rely exclusively on the past history of a place to explain paranormal occurrences, I believe some locations are "thin spots" between this and other worlds, dimensions, planes of existence, whatever you want to call them. Chapter 1's Court House Square and its surrounding buildings seem to be one such thin spot. Main Street Cafe seems to be another, albeit one that makes good coffee and great borscht.

Housed in a red-brick heritage home on the corner of McKenzie Avenue and Third Street in Revelstoke's downtown core, Main Street Cafe has been a popular breakfast and lunch spot since opening in 2003. A residential rental property for decades before being converted for commercial use, Main Street's cozy first-floor dining rooms and upstairs coffee lounge still retain the intimate look and feel of a private home. One wonders if that sense of comfort is what attracted the angry spirit whose early morning hauntings were, until recently, a fixture of Main Street Cafe.

*The Main Street Cafe is an integral part of
Revelstoke's community and downtown.*

The staff of Main Street Cafe were slow to recognize that they were sharing their workspace; initially, employee Rowan Tilley simply dismissed his creeping unease at working alone in the building. This unease persisted over time, eventually coalescing into the distinct feeling he wasn't alone in the shuttered restaurant. Tilley began obsessively checking doors to ensure they were locked.

His feelings of unease were validated early one morning when owner Shelly Klassen was working alone in the basement storage room.

"I had to run downstairs to get something, and I could hear somebody walking in the kitchen," she remembers. "I'd be down there and could hear somebody stomping up above. As soon as I came back upstairs, it would stop."

These footsteps happened to other employees as well, and the paranormal activity eventually became an accepted part of life for the staff at Main Street Cafe. No one thought twice about what was going on until events escalated.

"I had gone downstairs and I heard the stomping," remembers Klassen. "Then I heard a big crash."

Running upstairs, she found small pieces of kitchen equipment, including a zester and an espresso tamper, which had both been securely tucked away out of sight, scattered on the floor.

"Little things like that started happening," says Klassen. "And while I was in there by myself I could kind of see somebody walking by out of the corner of my eye when I was cooking."

Klassen wasn't the only one to start seeing, at least partially, the spirit of Main Street Cafe. Early one morning Rowan Tilley was in the restaurant alone doing prep work. Hearing unexplainable noises in the empty building had left him on edge, so when he made his way down to the cellar, he ensured that door was securely shut behind him.

When it was time to go back upstairs, Tilley turned to see, in the space between door and floor, a shadow gliding back and forth on the other side, and froze. He waited for the shadow to disappear, but forty minutes later it still silently paced on the other side of the door. Finally working up the nerve to face whatever awaited him on the other side, Tilley pulled open the door to see nothing there. Shaken, he returned upstairs to find the restaurant empty and the doors still locked.

The spirit also began to make itself known in other ways—most noticeably by playing with the front door sensor alarm. Klassen recalls the early morning shift when she and employee Christine Pearl witnessed the restaurant's front door alarm going haywire.

"It was first thing in the morning and I went out to the front, by the window on the Third Street side," remembers Klassen. "I was watering the plants, and I always have this thing about pushing chairs in at the table. So I pushed the chairs in. Then I went back in the kitchen, and we heard the door beep."

Klassen says Pearl "ran ... to the door, but there was nobody. It was pitch-black out."

Relocking the door, Pearl returned to the kitchen, only to have the alarm sound again almost right away. This time both women went out front to look and found the scene the same as before—with restaurant and winter streets still empty—but this time a single chair had been pulled away from the table.

After one final incident, in which Klassen heard the alarm sound while in the kitchen and heard it sound again with every step she took toward the locked front door, it was decided that the spirit couldn't stay.

"She's very unhappy that you are in this house"

Sometime in 2009, a psychic was brought in to advise the staff on what to do. The woman immediately saw the intruder sitting upstairs in a room that cafe patrons always found cold no matter what the thermostat said.

The psychic described the spirit as a very thin woman with long, straggly hair. She wasn't associated with the property but had been able to enter because, according to the psychic, "spirits will just come to a place that's open—that will let them in, so to speak." The psychic went on to tell staff: "She's very unhappy that you are in this house."

The female spirit was bitter that restaurant staff were cooking for and providing for people—inexplicably, she felt it should be her job, not theirs.

"According to the psychic, this woman absolutely hated men," says Klassen. "That's why she put the run on Rowan all the time and gave him this very uncomfortable feeling. Weird things would happen when he was here."

With the psychic's help, a ceremony was held to eject the spirit.

"I have never in my life experienced anything like that," says Klassen. "We helped her go. We had to basically 'lift' her, and she didn't want to go. The force that was on me—I had never felt anything so heavy."

As the thin woman began to pass over, the psychic observed two other spirits—a man and a young boy—coming to greet her. According to the psychic, the thin woman shunned the man and took the boy's hand.

Since that day, there have been no further reports of a presence at Main Street Cafe.

CHAPTER 12
Her Number One Fan

Though I enjoy a good scary story as much as anyone, this story—short as it is—is one of my favorites for the simple reason that it's not at all frightening; in fact, it's rather sweet. Many thanks to Mr. Haggerstone for taking the time to tell me about his family's life in Revelstoke in the 1960s. Thanks, too, to Ms. Fuoco, without whom this story would have been forgotten entirely.

Though over the years Revelstoke artist Winifred "Wyn" Haggerstone's depictions of local landscapes won her many fans—one of her sons remembers a couple from Alberta who would come to town every summer to purchase his mother's work—and she had gallery showings as far away as Whistler and Vancouver, Wyn always prized one fan's devotion over all others. The fan, a small boy, was special to Haggerstone not because of the compliments he paid her—in fact, the entire time she knew him the child never spoke a word—but because he came from so very far away to appreciate her work.

Wyn Haggerstone was born in London in 1922 and emigrated to Canada with her family at the age of five. It was following the family's move from Vancouver to the town of Pioneer that Wyn met her future husband, Ted, whom she wed in 1942, and it was there, in Pioneer, the couple would have their first children, Bruce and Jain.

The Haggerstones moved to Revelstoke in 1952, first settling into one of the wartime houses on East Fifth Street and relocating to a three-story home on McKenzie Avenue two years later. The family added two more members—twins John and James—in 1960, and it was several years afterward that Wyn took up painting.

The third floor of the McKenzie Avenue home became her studio; several easels stood in the middle of the room. Three of the four walls were hung with works both finished and unfinished, and the fourth was dominated by an enormous wooden desk, which Bruce had had to cut in half in order to fit up the small stairwell. The works themselves were usually a mixture of winter pastorals and mountain valleys covered in alpine flowers.

Like many Revelstoke families at that time, the Haggerstones rarely locked their doors, which one of the boys recalls would occasionally lead to some surprises on the winding staircase leading to the third floor.

"Sometimes there would be guys who wandered in there; transients, like—people who were traveling through," he says. "Sometimes she'd find somebody sleeping in the stairwell. She would never be too bothered by that, but my dad would have a fit, of course."

It was here, in her third-floor studio, where Wyn Haggerstone would come to paint once the children had gone to bed, and it was here where the boy—a spirit—having made his long journey from the land of the dead, would watch her.

Wyn came to expect and enjoy the visits from her long-time fan, even though she kept them a closely guarded secret from all but a handful of friends. In fact, with Wyn's passing in 2011, her close friend Annette Fuoco may be the last person who remembers.

"She used to tell me about him," says Fuoco. "He would come when it was all quiet and she was up there painting—a little fellow, around ten or twelve years old. He'd stand there watching her."

According to Fuoco, the child was said to be dressed in garb more appropriate for the 1850s than the 1950s: "She said he wasn't very big and was dressed in old-style pants and top. She saw that little guy for a long time. He was with her for years. She always said she enjoyed the company."

The current residents of the tall, white McKenzie Avenue home have never seen the child, or any other spirit for that matter, leaving us to wonder if he was drawn to the act of painting itself, Wyn Haggerstone, or a combination of the two, and whether or not the pair have renewed their acquaintance in the life that follows this one.

CHAPTER 13

Even the Nonbelievers

My favorite stories of the supernatural are almost invariably told by skeptics; there's something irresistibly compelling about a person who once held so firmly to a particular set of beliefs being forced to re-evaluate that worldview. The frustrating thing about stories told by skeptics is that they tend to over-analyze events after the fact and, by the time you hear their story, it may no longer be an accurate description of what occurred. The other danger, as shown here, is that after a while they might not want to discuss the event at all, which forces you to rely on third-party accounts. Thankfully, we have the account of Molly Quinn (not her real name), a reliable witness who was very helpful in providing information throughout the process of writing this book.

One fascinating aspect of the paranormal is how some will hope for an encounter their entire lives, jumping at shadows and squinting at every point of light in the night sky only to be disappointed, while others, firm in their belief of a world without mystery, will be presented with irrefutable evidence of the opposite.

Whether or not their experiences alter the belief structure of the resolutely rational witness is down to the person—some choose to forget the thing altogether, others methodically discount their senses until the memory is explainable through conventional means. David Quinn's experience in his former home near the corner of Third Street and Mackenzie Avenue, as told by his sister Molly, falls into the latter category.

It was in the summer of 2009 when Molly Quinn, her brother David, and friend Margot moved into the World War II–era house on West Third Street. Though ghosts were the last thing on anyone's mind, the trio's new landlord, Ronald Hall, casually informed them of their new home's reputation.

"Crazy Ronald said it was haunted by a woman, he knew her name, and so on," remembers Molly. "So I remember one night being home alone and saying out loud, 'I've got my own problems to deal with; I don't have time for this; don't come near me.' And it never did. It never bothered me."

Margot, however, wasn't so lucky. A bartender at local pub The Last Drop, she would finish work late, often arriving home at three or four in the morning.

"One night, she came home at maybe two or three in the morning," says Molly. "She went into the family room and shut the door."

The family room in the house has three entrances, two to the kitchen and one to a hallway off of which are three bedrooms. That morning, Margot ensured all three doors were soundly shut before picking up her guitar and beginning to play softly, something she would often do to unwind after work.

Molly goes on:

"As she played, the door from the hallway where the bedrooms are started shaking, like someone was holding on to the door handle and wiggling it back and forth."

Thinking she had woken someone, Margot began apologizing.

"She said something like, 'Oh crap, I'm super sorry, guys!' She thought it was my brother."

Margot put down her guitar and opened the hallway door to apologize to David.

"She realized that the door to my brother's room was wide open—he wasn't home. Neither was I. She was freaked out to the max."

David was next to experience something supernatural in the house, and his encounter, brief as it was, came as a shock to the hardened skeptic.

Molly explains:

"My brother is a complete atheist, not spiritual at all—he has no time for any of that hippy-dippy stuff. But he saw something."

One night, while sitting alone in his bedroom, David saw somebody walk by his door.

"His door was ajar ... he saw someone walking by in a furious manner, their hands balled into fists."

Thinking an intruder had come into their home, David sprang to his feet and searched the entire upstairs apartment, coming up empty.

"No one else was home," remembers Molly. "Hours later I got home from work and he's sitting there, as white as a dove. He told me I wouldn't believe what he saw."

Being the skeptic that he is, David has discounted the memory over time and refused to be interviewed for this story, but Molly is resolute in her recollection.

"He was a thirty-three-year-old guy at the time," she says, "and he was absolutely terrified."

CHAPTER 14

As Far Back as I Can Remember ... It Was Haunted

My interview with Roger Morrison took place in September 2012, only a few short months before he took his own life. Though it was not the only interview conducted for this story, it was the backbone on which the chapter was built, and in light not only of his death but also of the well-documented controversy that came after, I wrestled with whether or not I should cut it entirely. After months of consideration, I decided it should stay for the same reasons I had considered deleting it—out of respect for Roger and his family. During our interview, he was keen on telling not only the story of his boyhood home and its ghosts but also of his mother's love for that home and the way she carefully tended to its upkeep. Wherever he is, I hope he is pleased with the result.

Thanks to John Morrison for allowing us to take photographs of his house.

Roger Morrison was only two years old when his family first rented the Lundell House, moving from their apartments in the grand, neoclassical Birch Lodge on McKenzie Avenue. The four-bedroom, two-bathroom home near the northwest end of Ninth Street—with its gabled roof and screened-in side porch —was a step up for the young family, and Morrison's mother, Violet, took a great deal of pride in its upkeep.

"The house was a pride and joy for my mother, and she put a lot of work into it even though we didn't own it at first," said Morrison. "She felt that balanced out the things in the house that must accept us ... and my mother always felt the house accepted us.

"It's a little hard to explain," he adds. "But a lot of strange things happened over time, and as far back as I can remember, growing up, it was haunted."

Morrison, who died in 2012 at the age of fifty, remembered there being something unusual about a second-floor bedroom at the front of the house. While the room would eventually become Roger's when he grew older, as small children he and his brother were forbidden from using the room for anything other than storing their toys.

"That room was above the living room, and often at night you would hear ... the high heels of a woman walking around," he said. "I'm not sure of all the events because I was little, but my parents decided that nobody was staying in that room."

To make ends meet, Violet would often rent out a small side bedroom to boarders.

"One [boarder] was a guy named Syd Carey," remembered Morrison. "He was a funny guy ... used to work for the newspaper. He would always have change in his pocket and always be rattling it around. Years later after he passed away, you would still hear that sometimes in the hallway."

*As long as the Morrisons have lived in this house,
they've experienced paranormal events.*

The family pets, too, seemed aware of the unusual occurrences in the home.

"We always had cats and dogs," said Morrison. "Often, in the living room, all the animals would turn and look through the French glass windows to the hall and watch something pass by up the stairs. That would happen a lot."

One phenomenon that remained consistent throughout Morrison's life was the house's tendency to "disappear" certain items, only to have them reappear hours, days, even weeks later.

He explains:

"Friends would come over, they'd bring a record, say, and we'd listen to it then set it down to do some other things, and when it was time to go... there's no record. My friend would be freaking. How do you explain this to him? I'd say, 'Don't worry... it'll show up. It'll just show up,' and it would. Days later, there it would be."

Years later, when Morrison moved back into the home with his first wife, he found the spirits in the Lundell House had retained their mischievous nature.

"My former wife was doing Christmas cards one time— writing them all out," he said. "She'd put the whole set down, go through the list, and when she went to count them again there were three or four missing. Days later, they'd appear on a little side table."

Though such events were commonplace, Morrison never felt the house was in any way malevolent. His mother, who would eventually purchase the home from its previous owners, felt the same.

"My mother always believed it was haunted," remembered Morrison. "But she still wanted the house badly... it meant a lot to her.

"She always felt the house was just playing games with us. Nothing bad ever happened."

CHAPTER 15

The Rota House

The Rota House was home to three generations of my mother's family and, as I mentioned in the introduction, the catalyst for my starting this book. My mother had two brothers and three sisters, and when the family got together it wasn't unusual for them to tell ghost stories about the house they grew up in; from an early age, those stories ignited my interest in the supernatural. The house still stands, though so far as I know its paranormal activity has ceased.

On October 3, 1947, Samuel Rota—a twenty-four-year-old building supplies salesman and amateur baseball player—was crushed to death in a horrific workplace accident involving a logging truck. Rota's parents, Italian immigrants Joseph, forty-seven, and Mary, forty-one, were devastated by the loss; surviving family members say Mary wore the black of mourning every day thereafter until her death in 1964. Even in the full heat of summer, it was not uncommon for neighbors to see Mary, totally garbed in black, puttering around the Robson Street house that was home to four generations of the Rota family and now, some fifty years after her death and long after the last Rota passed through its doors, residents of that home believe Mary may still be there.

Cathy

My grandmother, Evelyn Martini, was one of Joseph and Mary's children and my mother, Cathy, was among the third generation of our family to live in the Rota house. Cathy's stories about growing up in a haunted house helped form the basis of my interest in the supernatural. Though many of the stories have faded from memory, she still recalls a few of the home's unexplained events.

"I remember a lot of times you'd get up in the morning and the coffee would be turned on," she says. "When we were teenagers, my mother used to have to go out of town sometimes, and my sister and I would be home alone together. We'd hear doors and dresser drawers opening and closing upstairs. The bathroom was upstairs, and when we had to go, we'd always go together. There was no fucking way we'd go up there alone."

Cathy's sister Julie also remembers those nights well:

"There was no wind or storm outside, but the bedroom door upstairs kept banging—open and closed, open and closed."

Julie was not yet born when her grandmother Mary passed away, but she remembers how Evelyn would sometimes attribute the house's strange activity to her mother's spirit.

"Mom used to tell us it was Grandma's spirit teasing us," remembers Julie. "We were still scared of it though."

Cathy says the activity experienced by the family—whether it was their grandmother's caprices or something else entirely—wasn't limited to the upstairs.

"Sometimes the lights would be on downstairs when we got up," she says, "and we knew we had shut them off."

Another time, the family heard their heavy wooden coffee table scraping across the living room floor.

"My mom was standing at the top of the stairs, shouting down if anyone was there," says Cathy with a laugh. "Because if it was a burglar they'd tell you."

"Your mom's house is haunted"

On rare occasions, visitors to the house would also have encounters with whatever unseen force lived there alongside the Martini family. Joe Martini (one of Cathy's and Julie's brothers), who, along with wife, Sue, raised their two children in the house, vividly recalls a friend who stayed on the living room couch for one night, and one night only.

"My friend Paul [Betts] needed a place to stay for a night," says Joe. "He was working up at Mica Creek [a small town some three hours north of Revelstoke] and he was coming south for some reason, so he asked if he could stay on our couch. That wasn't a problem."

He continues:

"Paul and I sat up talking for a while, then I went to bed. When Sue and I came downstairs in the morning, he was still sitting up on the couch. He hadn't touched the sheets or blanket I'd left out for him. He looked like shit ... I don't think he slept at all. When I asked him what was wrong, all he said was, 'I'm never staying here again.'"

Betts left shortly thereafter, and it would be decades before the two again crossed paths. When they did, Joe pressed his old friend for details about what had happened that night and was completely stonewalled by Betts.

"I hadn't seen him in almost thirty years," says Joe. "And all he says when I asked him is, 'Joe, your mother's house is haunted. That's all I'm gonna say.'"

Cathy says her mother never liked Betts, and she wonders if this has something to do with whatever fright he experienced that night.

"I know Mom hated him but I don't know why," she says. "She used to just hate it when he came to the house. One time she slammed the door in his face. Maybe my grandmother didn't like him either."

"There was light"

While the frightening aspects of haunting in the Rota house are noteworthy, they also had a much more comforting side, which has been experienced not only by the Rota and Martini families but also by another family who lived in the home years after those families left.

Julie Martini was the first person to experience this, back in the 1970s.

"I'm terrified of the dark," she says. "So when I was really little, my mother always kept the upstairs hall light on. One time, the light burned out and she couldn't afford to buy a new one right away, so the upstairs hallway was dark. I couldn't fall asleep."

Suddenly, as she lay there in bed, Julie says, a sliver of light from the hallway appeared underneath her bedroom door and she was finally able to fall asleep.

The next morning, Julie approached her mother.

"Hey Mom," she said, "who fixed the light last night?"

"Nobody," replied her mother.

"Yeah," said Julie, "it came on last night. That's how I went to sleep."

Her mother maintained that nobody had replaced the light, and took Julie upstairs to show her. Sure enough, the bulb was still burned out.

"To this day I don't know what happened," says Julie. "She hadn't fixed it, but all of a sudden there was light and I wasn't scared anymore."

"She was very comforting"

Beverly Armstrong was a teenager in the early 2000s when her family lived in the Rota House and, coincidentally, she occupied the same upstairs bedroom as had Julie. A typical teenager, the blond, blue-eyed Armstrong never gave much thought to spiritual matters and instead divided her time among school, friends, and her job at the local Denny's.

It was after a particularly long and draining shift at work that Armstrong had her first encounter with Mary, or whoever the spirit of the house may be.

"I worked till 11 p.m. that night," she recalls. "I came home, had my shower, and went to lie in bed. I wasn't feeling too well. When I was sick as a kid, my mom used to play with my hair, and it always made me feel better. Well, as I lay there, I felt someone start to play with my hair."

The feeling vanished when Armstrong sat up in bed. Looking around her room, there was no sign of her mother or anyone else, so she lay back down.

"It kept happening," she says. "And one time, I looked at the door and there's an elderly lady standing there."

Armstrong couldn't identify the woman, whom she described as slight of build and wearing a long, muumuu-like garment in dark blue or grey.

"It was weird ... I saw her, but then fell asleep right away, so I didn't have much of a chance to think about how she looked," she remembers. "She actually reminded me quite a bit of my grandmother."

Though that would be its only physical appearance, the mysterious figure would return to visit Armstrong several times over the two years she lived in the Rota House, always when she was most in need of care.

"It was always when I wasn't feeling well," she says. "When I was low, when I'd go to bed or wake up feeling sick, she would play with my hair and rub my shoulders. It didn't have to be late at night or anything, though—it would just depend on how I was feeling."

Sometimes the spirit, or entity, would speak to Armstrong as well.

"I would hear this voice—a woman's voice—talking to me, saying I was all right and that I was going to be okay. She was very comforting."

Armstrong was initially discomfited by these events, but she came to enjoy and even rely on them.

"There was nothing that she did to scare me, or anything like that. Basically, what she said to me was whatever a mother would do when you're not feeling good. She made me comfortable and calmed me down. It was soothing for me."

Whoever the spirit was, be it Mary Rota, Armstrong's own grandmother, or someone else entirely, her visits to Beverly stopped after the family moved out of the Rota House.

CHAPTER 16

Bocci's

If the Rota House is what started my interest in the supernatural, my own experiences at Bocci's are what finally caused me to take the subject more seriously. Even as a general skeptic and borderline atheist at the time, with reports coming from myself, my then-girlfriend, and other people who worked in the store, it was hard to deny that something weird was going on. Exactly what that was, I still don't know. Big thanks to now-owner of the Bocci's building Diane Mahoney for showing me around the renovated space—she's done a real service to the place and it has never looked better.

The building affectionately referred to as Bocci's has been a grocery store for nearly eighty years. Almost everyone who lives, or has lived, in the area surrounding the corner of Fourth Street and Victoria Road has a story about shopping in the small corner store known first as City Groceteria, then Vince's, and finally, Bocci's. What many of them don't know is that some of the people who have worked in the store or lived in the apartment above have stories much different than those told in the neighborhood.

From 2000 to 2006, I worked as a grocery clerk at Bocci's Groceteria. From 2002 to 2004, I also rented the upstairs apartment. This story begins around that time, with the most recent incident taking place nine years later, in January 2011. I suppose you can take that to mean the story isn't over yet.

Throughout its eighty years, this building has housed many businesses, but it's most wellknown as Bocci's.

A Creeping Unease

The apartment above Bocci's was my first—I graduated in June 2001 and paid the security deposit on my new home just after my nineteenth birthday in March of the following year.

The place was enormous—once upon a time it had served as two separate apartments, meaning it now had two full bathrooms and a total of five bedrooms. The amount of space was completely overwhelming, and I went about filling it with all the toys you'd expect from an employed nineteen-year-old male: big-screen television, stereo, beer fridge, foosball table, and so on. Each room had a "theme, " if you can call it that— TV room, computer room, games room—except for one room at the very top of the stairs. The smallest room in the apartment, with a door in the closet that led to the attic; nothing ever "stuck" there, and it became a storage space and crash pad for passed-out party guests.

At first, the only door I made sure to close in the apartment was the outside door at the bottom of the stairs. The other door at the bottom led into the back room of Bocci's and was always bolted from the other side. After locking my front door, I'd leave every other one in the apartment, including my bedroom, wide open and fall asleep with music playing on the stereo in the living room.

Over the course of the next month, I found myself uncomfortable sleeping with the door open. There was no reason for it, but all the same I began closing the door before going to bed. Not long after, something started to bother me about music playing in the empty living room and I started turning that off before closing the door. Finally, I reached a point when it wasn't possible to sleep unless the door was also locked. At this point, despite an abiding love of spooky stories and horror films, the idea of something supernatural taking place didn't even enter my mind. In fact, I thought I was going nuts.

Then one night as I lay in bed, my eyes closed, I heard what sounded like wine glasses clinking. That wasn't cause for alarm— the Canadian Pacific Railway's train yard is a stone's throw away, so I assumed the movement of a train was shaking the dishes in my cupboard. Then I began to hear other sounds—silverware on a table, light music, and—finally—voices speaking indistinctly; it sounded like a grand dinner party taking place in my apartment. I bravely kept my eyes closed, rolled over, and stayed that way until I fell asleep. That was the beginning.

In the following days and months, I began to hear something often reported by people who feel their homes are haunted—footsteps in the night. In this case, they always came from the store downstairs. Now, it wasn't unusual for the owners of Bocci's to stick around after hours—sometimes to clean, sometimes to drink coffee and shoot the breeze in the back room—so I was used to hearing their sounds: footsteps, voices, the ringing of the front-door alarm when it opened and closed.

Except there were nights when I'd hear these sounds quite late, and when asked the next morning, the bosses would tell me everyone had left the store by 9 p.m.

Then, on Halloween 2002, I was approached at a house party by a woman who used to live in the apartment.

"Hey, you live above Bocci's now, right?" she said. "Have you had anything strange happen up there?"

When I asked her what she meant by strange, she went on to describe the same progression of emotions I had experienced after moving in—from comfort, to unease, to full-on paranoia. She said the roommates she had lived with "didn't even like being in the apartment by themselves." She also said her children had invisible friends they'd play with—but only in the room at the top of the stairs.

Eventually, I got a roommate myself, and despite not telling her a single thing about the strange feelings the apartment inspired, she too went through the same cycle and, after a while, didn't like being there alone either, particularly at night.

By the time I moved away in 2004, things had quieted down so much in the apartment that I'd almost written off the things I'd experienced after moving in. Then one night a few months later, I was in a coffee shop with friends when the young woman who rented the apartment after me came up and asked to speak privately. Once we were away from the table she said, "You used to live above Bocci's, right? Did you ever have anything strange happen up there?"

By now you can guess the rest of the conversation.

A year later, the apartment was again vacant and I was in the back room of the store counting up the day's receipts. The sound of heavy bass started coming from next door, which was odd since the neighbors had come by earlier in the week to let us know they'd be out of town. Assuming their kids were having a party in their absence, I went back to work, only to stop again after remembering the kids had gone with them too. Rising from my desk, I realized the heavy bass sound wasn't coming from next door—it was coming from the empty apartment upstairs.

Moving toward the door that connected the Bocci's back room to the first-floor landing of the apartment, I could hear the sound move as well—that strange, heavy thumping coming closer and closer. My first thought was maybe the boss had left the apartment door unlocked while he was showing tenants around and a local hobo had wandered in—Revelstoke is a small place, but even so we have a few derelicts drifting around. After opening the door between the store and the apartment, I could see the manager had remembered to lock the door behind him, meaning there was no way anyone could have entered afterward. Just then, the thumping stopped, and there was a footfall on the part of the stairs I couldn't see. I slammed the door shut, double-locked it, and bravely got out of there at top speed.

That was in 2005, and it would be my last interaction with whatever is going on at Bocci's for almost six years; the store was sold to new owners in early 2006, and I ended up relocating to the southern tip of Vancouver Island just over a year later. It was during a visit home in January 2011 that I had what has been my last strange encounter with the building.

A Blue Flash

While out for a walk one night, I found myself standing across Fourth Street from what had been our store. The new owners hadn't lasted long, and now the lower part of the building was under construction, to be turned into a spa and yoga studio. It was cold that night, but I stood there for almost an hour thinking about the six years we had spent running Bocci's and everything it had meant to us.

A burst of light—like a camera flash—in one of the darkened upstairs windows startled me from my reverie. It was a bright blue and appeared to come from what was once my living room. For a moment I stood there wondering why someone would take pictures in the dark and was just about to conclude the whole thing had been my imagination when the flash repeated itself—in every window of the apartment, simultaneously. I very quickly turned and made my way home.

A New Start

Upon beginning this project in 2012, I approached the current owner of Bocci's, Diane Mahoney, to see if her experience with the store and apartment above had been at all similar to my own. Mahoney was happy to talk about her time in the building, which she had so lovingly rebuilt into Welwinds Therapeutic Spa and Tea Bar, but confessed she had had no experiences to match my own.

It was strange for me to see how radically the interior of the building had been transformed and how much different it felt. While my early experiences in Bocci's were happy ones, they became stranger and more frightening over time and my view of the building changed accordingly; walking into Welwinds, I felt that apprehension melt away. Whether whatever spirits are in the building are pleased with its transformation or they've simply moved on, Bocci's now feels the way it did at the beginning: warm, welcoming, and happy.

That said, one throwback to my days in the apartment still remains: despite Mahoney having rebuilt the entire upstairs, including knocking down the walls and changing the entire floor plan, there is still one room that feels the same, a room in which Mahoney had a new marble countertop installed, only to find it inexplicably cracked one morning soon after. That room, still the smallest in the apartment, is right at the top of the stairs and—despite Mahoney's efforts to use it for other purposes—still wound up being storage space.

Nothing, she says, has ever quite "stuck" there.

CHAPTER 17

My Mother's House

The idea of telling my own stories worried me a bit at first—after all, I have a straight job that doesn't involve me talking up this kind of thing, and I wasn't sure if people would think I was a kook. Telling people about Bocci's was one thing—I wasn't even close to the only person who'd experienced something out of the ordinary there—but opening up and talking about things that had happened to me alone? Now that was scary stuff. Eventually, though, I decided that the people who mattered already knew how kooky I was and anyone who didn't could either get with the program or hit the bricks. As for my mother's house itself, I believe that whatever was in there is gone—the house, particularly the basement, feels ... lighter now. The shadows? Well, from time to time I still see them and they still see me, but I'm not the person I was and they keep their distance.

My own encounters with the supernatural while growing up in Revelstoke were limited; Chapter 18, "Green Light," tells of my most dramatic experience, which happened while I was in my teens. That was my final childhood encounter with the supernatural, and it wasn't until moving into the apartment above Bocci's in 2002 (see Chapter 16) that my awareness again expanded to planes beyond the visible. Until then, every single paranormal experience I had took place in my mother's house.

Invisible Hands

My first encounter took place when I was perhaps four or five years old, and is one of my earliest memories. I remember lying in my room one night and suddenly feeling as though I wasn't alone. This seemed unlikely—my parents were both downstairs and my grandmother, who watched after me while they were at work, had gone home hours ago—but the feeling would not go away. Then, all of a sudden, I felt warm hands on my back underneath my pajama shirt; the hands slowly stroked up and down my spine in a reassuring fashion for perhaps a minute before disappearing. When they'd gone, I spun around in bed to catch sight of whoever or whatever had been the cause, but my bedroom door was closed and there was no one to be seen. Because I was never frightened, the incident never came to my parents' attention, but every now and again it drifts back to me and I am no more able to explain it now than I was at the time.

The Breath in the Dark

Like many teenagers, I adopted the family basement as my own and consequently spent most of my time there, either watching movies or playing video games with friends. At some point, an old hide-a-bed sofa we couldn't be bothered to throw away ended up down there, too, and with it came the bright idea of making the basement my room.

Our basement was divided into two halves; the first, unfinished half, was located at the bottom of the stairs. This was where our furnace and hot water tank were located, and it also functioned as a storage area. A doorway separated this area from the second half, my hideaway, which was paneled in wainscoting and had an atrocious shag carpet.

Late one night, while lying on the enormously uncomfortable pull-out sofa bed, I heard footsteps approaching in the dark. My eyes were closed but I assumed it was my mother, who could be a bit of an insomniac, quietly coming downstairs to check on me. She and my sister were the only other two people in the house, and my sister, bless her, never does anything quietly. My mother stood there for maybe five or ten minutes, her breathing the only sound, then turned and walked away; shortly thereafter I fell asleep.

In the morning, I approached my mother and asked why she had come downstairs.

She hadn't, and neither had my sister. That was the last night I slept in the basement.

Shadows

The most frightening paranormal experience of my life came in May 2012, shortly after beginning work on this book, and it wasn't until afterward that I realized it bore an unmistakable resemblance to another incident from my childhood. As it turns out, I am no stranger to Shadow People.

It all started after returning home from my first research trip to Revelstoke. I was back at my day job chatting with our then-receptionist, Almira. Our office at the time was an enormous space—some 1,500 square feet divided into six offices, a meeting room, and a kitchen—but on that particular day Almira and I were the only two at work.

While relating some of the stories I had thus far collected for my book, I saw, in the office directly behind her desk, an all-black head slowly tilt out from behind a rack full of coats. It stayed there for a few seconds before tilting back behind the rack, and though it had only been visible from the corner of my eye, I could clearly see it had no features—like a shadow.

Despite my taste for ghost stories and horror movies, I have always been a strictly rational person, and while these things brought me an enormous amount of enjoyment, until that head poked out there was never a question of the supernatural being anything more to me than another kind of entertainment. A panic set in and color seemed to bleed from what had previously been a bright spring day, but with great effort I managed to ignore what I'd seen and keep talking. Eventually, my vision brightened and I told myself it had all been my imagination.

Two weeks later, that illusion was taken away from me when the shadow appeared again, this time around 8 a.m. on another lovely spring morning. My wife goes to work earlier than I, and so I was still lying in bed enjoying the sunlight streaming through our blinds when I noticed something out of the corner of my left eye; someone was standing just behind me. The problem with this was that the head of our bed sits against the east wall of our bedroom and with night tables on either side it is not technically possible to stand where I felt whatever it was was standing. Turning my head, I saw a shadowy figure looming over me—shaped like a man but with no features—and before I could react, the creature fell across me in the bed. When it touched me, I felt as though I had touched a live wire—something like electricity coursed through my body—and I lost consciousness. When I awoke again half an hour later, the whole thing seemed like a dream, except for a feeling of extreme fatigue and depression that had come over me.

When these feelings finally cleared a week later, following an eruption of terrible sadness and anger, I remembered this wasn't the first time such a thing had happened to me.

The same grandmother who used to babysit my sister and me had a taste for gossip magazines, so there was always a spare *Star* and/or *Enquirer* magazine sitting about, which, sometime around the age of ten, began to pique my interest. Not having any idea who people like Burt Reynolds or Loni Anderson were, I was nonetheless intrigued by their slowly crumbling marriages or drug addictions, mostly because I had no idea how these things related to real life. In one of these magazines, I happened across an article about "opening yourself to spirit" and "drawing upon the power of the earth for strength," and because I was cross-pollinating my tabloid habit with a fondness for superhero comics, doing both these things sounded rather appealing.

The article described a visualization exercise I no longer recall that I attempted one night while lying in bed. Nothing happened, much to my disappointment, and I lay there on my back looking at the red digital readout of my alarm clock. Around 8:30 p.m. I began to notice what looked like bats circling in the darkness above my bed. At first I wasn't alarmed—I assumed my mother had absentmindedly left the screen off my window —but when I attempted to rise and call someone for help with removing the offending critters, I found myself unable to move.

Above me, in what little streetlight filtered through my curtains, I watched the shadowy things flit back and forth. I was still unable to move or make a sound. Finally, the things changed direction, first arcing upward toward the ceiling before diving down toward where I lay helpless. The creatures passed into my chest, first one, then the other, and my entire body came alive with what felt like electricity. Shortly thereafter I lost consciousness and didn't wake again till morning.

Between grades four and five, I went from being an outgoing, extroverted child to an unhappy, introverted one, and though I can no longer pin down the date of my encounter with the shadow bats, it would not surprise me to learn that this was the dividing moment. The aftereffects of my most recent encounters have shown me in stark detail how damaging contact with these creatures can be.

It wasn't until 2013 that I met someone else who had seen them, a man who had encountered the shadows while struggling against depression and a relapse into drug addiction. Not a particularly religious person, he nonetheless found himself at wit's end, in a church praying for help with his struggle; as he put it, "I had to try something." As the man prayed for deliverance, two creatures he described as being "like bats" erupted from his chest and abruptly disappeared an arm's length away. Though he still fights depression on a daily basis, the man did not relapse, and the day the bats left him marked a positive turning point in his life.

Just as with the green light described in the chapter of the same name, it was comforting to know someone else had shared this strange experience, though it got me no further in understanding exactly what happened, or why.

CHAPTER 18

Green Light

The story of the green light is one of those bizarre personal recollections that don't quite "fit" and so tend to fade until something jogs my memory. In that respect, it's similar to the stories from Chapter 17, "My Mother's House"—most of those things were buried in my mind and it wasn't until I actually made an effort to look for them that I was able to remember them in full. As I mention in later chapters, this seems to be a common feature of truly supernatural phenomena—the mind actively seeking to forget what doesn't fit into its established framework of reality.

My most dramatic and verifiable personal encounter with the unknown took place on New Year's Eve, though exactly which one is still very much up for debate. My memory of the event itself is still reasonably sharp, but the difficulty begins when trying to place it in the timeline of my life. The friend who witnessed the event with me—Aaron Irmen—believes it couldn't have been before 1998, but other people we saw that night are certain it was earlier. Whatever the case, Aaron and I would have been teenagers at the time of the event and, in true teenage fashion, we celebrated the New Year by playing video games and cracking wise. Our teenage years not being rambunctious ones, the only stimulants we had helped ourselves to that evening were caffeine and sugar, so our recollections of what followed cannot be questioned on the basis of intoxication.

As is usual in Revelstoke around that time of year, snow had been falling heavily all night, and at one point, possibly around 3 a.m., we decided it would be a good idea to shovel my mother's driveway. This wasn't an altruistic decision as much as it was one born of the jitteriness associated with too much off-brand cola.

Outside it was cold, still, and bright, the fresh snow everywhere reflecting the light of a dozen street lamps. We set into the wet, almost slushy, snow with our shovels, but even with two of us it was slow going. My mother's modest driveway took an hour to clear, and we finished at 4 a.m. Though we disagree on exactly what year the event took place, my and Aaron's memories of that night agree up to this point; from here on, our recollections diverge and the description given is a synthesis of both our memories.

At four in the morning, I was standing next to my mother's car in our driveway and Aaron was standing at the sidewalk's edge, looking down an empty Third Street; snow was piled chest high in windrows down the center of the road and there wasn't a sound—even the nearby rail yard had gone quiet for the time being. It was in that silence that the light came—to me from above Mount Revelstoke to the northeast, to Aaron from over Boulder Mountain in the northwest. It began as a small point of neon green light above the mountain, just a pinprick in the night sky, and then it flashed brightly.

Before we had time to react, the light flashed again, and this time both of us were bathed in green, but not as though illuminated by a floodlight; rather, it was as though the very air around us had turned a brilliant neon. Though it couldn't have lasted more than a few seconds, I distinctly remember watching my hand move through this strange, new air as I tried to make sense of it. The light was gone before we could react, leaving Aaron and me staring at one another in confusion. We left the shovels where they were and went back inside.

Though we've talked about it infrequently over the years, neither of us has any idea what happened that night. Certainly, we both remember it taking place very quickly but nothing beyond that—neither of us recall the changing air having any physical effect or feeling, and we were both so preoccupied by the light that if anything else happened it went totally unnoticed, at least by us.

For a long time, Aaron and I believed we were the only witnesses to this kind of event, but then in 2014, during the course of researching this book, I found another.

In 2002, Clare Mount, whose haunted house story appears in Chapter 19, "In the Mountain's Shadow," was in the middle of a three-day bicycle trip with friends through Australia's Blue Mountains.

"I was in grade eight," she remembers. "We were lying in our sleeping bags in the middle of a field when this huge, green—I thought it was a comet—came down. I thought it was gonna hit. It was the only moment in my life I thought the whole world was going to end."

Before the light could touch down, Clare hid under her sleeping bag and braced for what she believed to be her final moments. While an impact came, it was hardly the apocalypse she had anticipated.

"I closed my eyes and a huge wave went through my body," she said. "I was screaming and all my friends were asking me what was wrong with me."

Clare opened her eyes to find the green light gone and her world unchanged; what's more, none of her friends had observed the mysterious fireball or felt its shockwave. For years, just as with Aaron and me, Clare wondered if she had imagined the entire episode. Though we now all feel safe in saying what we experienced was genuine, we are no closer to understanding the green light, its source, or why we could see it when others did not.

CHAPTER 19

In the Mountain's Shadow

This story fascinates me for two reasons: one being that it contains what I believe to be an encounter—albeit in dream form—with Shadow People, making it the first such story I've found in Revelstoke. Clare Mount did not use the phrase "Shadow People" in relating her experience, but after reading her description of the entity she encountered, not to mention the run of bad luck that followed, one is hard-pressed to call it anything but. The other thing that fascinates me is where it takes place—the house Clare now calls home previously belonged to a long-time Revelstoke resident who happened to be stepfather to a friend of mine while we were growing up. During my teen years, we spent a considerable amount of time in that house at all hours of the night and none of us ever experienced a single instance of paranormal phenomena. That said, we never experienced it anywhere else, either, which suggests to me this kind of activity could be present in many places where residents are simply unable to see or feel it.

Thanks to Clare and Chelsea for the interview, Michelle for making it happen, and Salon Safari for letting me conduct an interview in-house in the middle of a workday.

The activity described in this chapter all took place very close to the time of Clare's interview and so does not encompass all the activity that has happened in the home, or may happen in the future. Like others in this book, this story is still very much being written.

Read enough accounts of paranormal occurrence and you begin to recognize a through-line: phenomena which, regardless of whether you're looking at a haunting, UFO abduction, or Sasquatch sighting, appear to be inextricably entwined with the supernatural. One such phenomenon, amply demonstrated in the pages of this book, is the disturbance of animals; Turk Wilson's collie dogs barking at the man in the field, Roger Morrison's cats and dogs turning their heads in unison to watch something unseen make its way up the stairs, the Verlaine family cat's edginess upon moving into Holten House—these are only a few examples of household pets' ability to perceive things beyond the edge of human understanding. Often this is one of the first and only indications someone has of paranormal activity in their home. But for the people named above, it merely marked the beginning of their experiences. So, too, for Clare Mount.

Mount is a twenty-something Australian expatriate living in Revelstoke who purchased her Moss Street home in late 2013. The house, a one-and-a-half-story A-frame built in 1932, sits at the back of a long, grassy lot situated in the shadow of Mount McKenzie, not far from the Illecillewaet River.

"It's funny," says Mount. "When we first looked at that place, I was in there with my mom and I told here there was something in there. I could feel something else in there. She could kind of feel it too, but obviously, I didn't want to make that my reason not to buy a house."

After moving in, the feeling never quite went away but never got stronger, either, and it wasn't until her dog began to behave strangely that Mount's suspicions about the house were confirmed.

"When we first moved in, my dog acted funny in one spot," she remembers. "She would be sleeping in the lounge and wake up suddenly. She would look up, then get up, back away, and growl. It was like somebody was coming toward her ... always in that one corner."

Mount's family has a long history of spiritual sensitivity, and so rather than being afraid, her first instinct was to try to clear the home via smudging, a ritual that involves burning and dispersing the smoke of herbs such as sage or sweetgrass.

"I had a different roommate in there at the time, and she said she felt a different presence or something," Mount recalls. "We ended up saging her room, too, because she was uneasy about it."

For a time, this seemed to have the desired effect, as her dogs —and roommate—slept easier.

"Nothing happened after I saged ... well, maybe it did. I don't know ... I had lots of people in the house ... five roommates. When something happened, I just blamed it on someone else."

"Only a dream"

It wasn't until months later that Mount had a supernatural encounter she couldn't ascribe to pedestrian causes—something that had real-world consequences despite the fact that, at first blush, it seemed like something easy to write off as "only a dream."

"I had an experience in March [2014], two weeks after a Reiki appointment," she remembers. Reiki is a spiritual practice through which a practitioner distributes life-energy, or qi, throughout the body of another to help them achieve physical, emotional, and spiritual balance.

"I went for the Reiki because I wanted to open up further. Then as soon as I opened up I had...I don't know; it was like some sort of weird dream where I feel like...it was real. In it, I was downstairs in my house, and as I came up the stairs, it was waiting at the top, in my room. Some dark shadow came and put me on the ground."

Mount describes an entity resembling a "Dementor"—a hooded, dread-inducing shadow creature that drains the vitality of those unfortunate enough to be near it—from the *Harry Potter* series.

"It didn't touch me but I could feel it...like it was holding me. There was a powerful force behind it, like a shock wave. I cried out—screamed—and woke up in my bed. I could still feel the energy from it. I thought to myself that something had tried to hurt me."

Shaken, she called her family's spiritual guide back in Australia and explained what had just happened.

"It was super intense," she says. "That was my first scary experience, so I told her about it and she told me I was too open—that I was letting too much in. Since then I've tried to control … my spiritual development … a little better and whatever it was, hasn't come back."

Though the entity wasn't able to touch Mount, it seems as though its presence left a mark—shortly after the experience she suffered a run of bad luck, losing her dog to an animal attack and then herself suffering prolonged illness, culminating in a bout of shingles. Her recovery marked the beginning of another quiet period in the home, which lasted from late March until a morning in September 2014.

The Record Player

"It was September 24, like four in the morning," says Mount. "I woke up to a super loud noise."

Rising from bed, Mount shook off her heavy sleep and strained to hear what the sound was and where it was coming from. After a moment, she recognized it was music, coming from downstairs.

"It was Bob Marley playing," she recalls. "I was ready to go smack my roommate for doing that at four in the morning."

It was then she recalled her roommate was out of town and she was alone in the house.

Rising from bed, she padded across the darkened room to the stairwell, her eyes adjusting to the dark as she scanned constantly for another sign of the shadowy being that had accosted her in March.

At the bottom of the stairs, she looked toward the closed door to her roommate's room, which was now unmistakably the source of the sound.

"The record player was blaring out of his room. I didn't know what to do," says Mount. "My roommate has a record player ... you need to put the needle down and press the button to start it. It's not like it could start by accident."

"I opened up the door. The record was spinning. Bob Marley was playing. I didn't turn it off, didn't even go in. I just closed the door and went back upstairs."

In the morning, the music was gone, the record had stopped spinning, and the needle had returned to the upright position, but the strange energy in Mount's home wasn't finished.

Bruises

A week later, Mount was awakened by her dogs at the same time as the music had played.

"It was four in the morning," she remembers. "I thought, 'Okay dogs, we don't go outside and pee at four in the morning. What are you doing?'"

She reluctantly got up and went downstairs to let the dogs out.

"I opened up the door and both of them bolted outside into the dark, which was a weird thing for them to do."

When the dogs finally came back, Mount let them in and returned to bed.

"This is the weird bit. I had gotten under my blankets and then ... Well, I went into a trance kind of thing. I knew what I was doing but couldn't stop myself. It was like my body had been taken over by a different source. I was made to do things and I couldn't stop it. I just had to go with the flow and not be afraid of it, I guess. It was weird."

Under this strange influence, Mount collected her blankets and took them downstairs, where she lay down in the middle of the floor. It was then that she was seized by something she could not see.

"Something grabbed me right here," she says, gesturing at her right thigh. "I ended up having bruises—I have pictures of them."

The unseen force held Mount in place for what seemed like an eternity.

"I knew it was happening but couldn't stop it. I just waited for it to end. I don't know how long it was."

Finally, the presence seemed to dissipate and Mount returned to bed, where she pulled the covers over her head.

CHAPTER 20

A Haunted Life

Barb Johnson is an old family friend who gave me a great interview, providing not only the small handful of stories in this book in which her name appears, but also a number of fascinating anecdotes not long enough to be turned into full-fledged chapters. She seems to be among a small group of people for whom paranormal interactions are the rule rather than the exception, though she doesn't make a point of sharing such things unless asked.

One inconvenient thing about supernatural experiences is that they rarely happen when you're ready for them, and they often occur at your weakest point—be it when you're barely awake, ill, or huddled alone in the dark. Such things are likely not meant to frighten you, but they can have that effect, though the opposite can also be true; sometimes an encounter with a spirit can help lift you up from the place you've fallen and give you hope. Over the course of her life, Barb Johnson has experienced, among other things, the specter of her dead grandmother, disembodied voices, and, most dramatically, her encounter with the white light—all of which have frightened and reassured her in equal measure.

Past Experience

Johnson, a lifelong Revelstoke resident, is no stranger to the paranormal—at twelve years old she saw her recently deceased grandmother standing outside her grandparents' home.

"After my grandmother died, my friend Dina and I went up to my gram and grandpa's house with my dad," she recalls. "My dad was in the kitchen and we were in a back bathroom that faced my grandparents' raspberry canes ... having a cigarette. At the age of twelve—can you imagine?"

In order to keep the smell of smoke from drifting inside, Johnson recalls, the children were blowing it out the window.

"We're sticking our heads out the window, right? And my sister comes around outside the window and asks for a puff. So I gave her one, and as I looked beyond her ... there was my grandmother."

Barb says Dina saw her as well, and the two girls stood rooted to the spot.

"She was as solid as you or me—none of this filmy ghost shit. It was like looking at a regular person. She was walking through the canes and looked right at me. Then she disappeared around the corner of the house. Dina and I went screaming out of the bathroom. I'm fifty-nine years old, and we still talk. Every now and again, I'll ask her if she remembers. Boy, does she ever."

Years later, following the death of her second husband, Johnson would have another brush with the unseen.

"I was sitting downstairs in my basement playing computer games," she recalls. "I was a mess. Thinking, 'Oh my

God, what's going to happen to me now?' and that kind of thing. It was terrible."

As she sat there, Johnson heard what sounded like two male voices coming from a broken set of computer speakers.

"These speakers were not working… they hadn't worked in a long time," she says. "They were just sitting there, not even connected. I didn't care about much right then, so I never bothered to throw them out."

Johnson says the two voices were tinny and garbled by static, like conversation over a CB radio.

"You really had to listen, but I listened all right," she says. "Sound coming from speakers that don't work? You listen."

"What's the road look like up ahead?" the first voice asked.

"Well, I don't know," came the reply. "It's kind of bumpy but it should be okay."

After this exchange, the speakers again went quiet and Johnson sat in stunned silence. After a time, although she had no idea where they had come from, she decided that the words had been meant for her.

"What I can gather," she says, "is that my road was gonna be bumpy for a while, which it had been, but it was all gonna be okay in the end. And you know? It was."

The White Light

At the time of her encounter with the white light, Johnson was recently divorced and living alone in Hideaway Trailer Court, a collection of several dozen mobile homes tucked away behind Southside Grocery Market.

"After my divorce, I had moved up to my brother's place for a couple months until I decided what to do," remembers Johnson. "Then I bought a trailer in Hideaway. Number 34."

The first few months in her new home were unremarkable, until one night she was startled out of a dead sleep.

"I woke up to these huge, bright lights outside," she recalls. "They were incredible. And there was this hum. You know when you go past a transformer on a street and you can hear a humming? Like that, except it was so loud it was almost deafening."

A look at the yard for trailer number 34 offers no possibilities as to where this anomaly could have come from—no lights or electrical equipment of any kind—and to add to the mystery, not one of Johnson's neighbors experienced the same phenomenon.

"All I know," she says, "is that there was this incredible bright white light in my side yard, between my trailer and the neighbor's. I was too afraid to open the blinds and see what it was. I don't even know when it happened—I was too afraid to get out of the bed and look at the clock."

Johnson estimates that the whole incident lasted, at most, a minute, though she can't be sure.

"I tried hard to ignore it," she says. "I thought, 'Oh my God!' and put my head under the blankets."

CHAPTER 21
The Children See

The family who gave me these stories was extremely helpful with not only this chapter but others as well, and they deserve a major thank-you for letting a stranger in on something they considered very private. It'll be fascinating to see if the children retain their sensitivity to the supernatural as they get older.

Though it is generally accepted that children are more open to paranormal experiences, there is no clear consensus about why; one popular theory holds that the impressionable nature and inexperience of youth allows a child to accept strange happenings without having them clash with a deeply entrenched belief system, as is so often the case with adults. Whatever the case, it does seem as though children see more of the astral plane than adults do—even those of us with an aptitude for sensing the energy of worlds beyond our own.

Though she doesn't consider herself psychic, Theresa Proud is no stranger to the unusual. As a child in rural Nebraska she witnessed mysterious orbs of light drifting around her family home, and years later was witness to a sighting of the legendary Saune-min Giant in Saunemin, Illinois, and so she has never been overly concerned when experiencing the supernatural in her home.

"Just within the past couple of years I've had weird feelings," she says. "But I always thought it's more me being eerie on my own."

Theresa's husband, Steve, has been attending school in a neighboring town during the week, which means she's often home alone at night with her two children, Peter and Andrew.

"Every once in a while, I get feelings like someone's around. It's not an uncomfortable feeling for me," she explains. "I have a lot of people who have passed on who were very close to me. Sometimes I get that feeling and immediately one of them comes to mind. It's not like I'm searching for who it could be—I have the feeling, and right away it's like I know."

Theresa says if these feelings were the only indication of presence in her home, she would be unlikely to have paid them much heed. Her children soon began to notice something un-usual, however, and, for Peter at least, in far more vivid fashion.

"One day I was home alone with Andrew," Theresa recalls. "I was in the kitchen, he was in the living room—the two are di-vided by a window—and I clearly heard a male voice say hello. It sounded like he was in my kitchen, right off the door. Andrew heard it too, because he looked up at me through the window."

On its own, hearing the greeting was not particularly un-usual, says Theresa.

"My neighbor always comes by, and he doesn't really knock; he'll just open the door and say something," she explains. "So I went around the corner to check the front door, and there was nobody there. We have two doors—exterior and interior. If someone had come in and out quickly, we'd have heard at least one of them."

Peter's encounter happened in his room, which Theresa has always felt is a little bit "off."

"I have to walk by it to get to my bedroom," she says. "And you know those places where you don't want to walk by in the dark—you walk as fast as you can? That's this room."

Theresa says her own feelings were confirmed when Peter was four years old.

"He would wake up and tell me there was a man in his room. He always said the man was dressed in underwear and socks. It didn't happen for a long time. It was maybe a year before he stopped talking about it."

The boy was never frightened by his visitor, who he says would stop in the doorway, wave at him, and then walk off through his shelf and wall.

As have so many others faced with the inexplicability of the supernatural, Theresa and Steve Proud's children have taken these events in stride, and the family continues to live comfortably in their home to this day. Though many would deny the reality of those experiences, or demand they make some kind of cohesive sense, Theresa has chosen to accept them without worrying about an explanation.

"I've reached a point in my life," she says, "when I have experienced enough inexplicable things that I just accept it's happening. Whatever it is."

CHAPTER 22

Northern Lights

Apart from contributing to this particular chapter, Terry Lott—a man well versed in the night sky—was able to provide a lot of help when other stories of strange lights came up. While my spiritual beliefs—such as they are—differ greatly from Terry's, I do very much believe he saw what he says he did. Despite being a night owl for much of my life, I have yet to properly see the northern lights, and after hearing what Terry had to say, I confess to being a little bit jealous.

In the eons before we knew it to be a function of the natural world, countless witnesses mistook the Aurora Borealis for a supernatural phenomenon. In Norse mythology, the Aurora Borealis was said to be light reflected from the armor of Valkyries as they rode across the night sky; the Gunai people of Australia's Gippsland believed the lights to be the campfires of the dead.

While we now understand it to be the result of charged particles entering the earth's atmosphere, some still approach the Aurora Borealis with a sense of wonder and a hope that it may yet offer deeper mysteries. Amateur astronomer Terry Lott is one such person, and on a night in the 1990s, the Aurora Borealis did not disappoint.

"I got my first telescope in 1995," he recalls. "I spent hours out there, but it wasn't until 1998 I saw something really weird."

Lott was out one night, stargazing as usual.

"The northern lights were starting to form," he says. "First I noticed them above Mount McPherson, then I noticed—how would I describe it?—a cloudy band all the way across the sky above me, from McKenzie in the northwest to Boulder in the southwest. It wasn't solid, because I could see stars through it."

Lott said the band appeared to be part of the Aurora Borealis save for the fact that it wasn't colored.

"It was...like a light," he explains. "A band of light. It was enormous, you know, like...when you're looking at the sky, that's a lot of sky. The funny thing was, for the northern lights to go from one horizon to another across the sky this way is unusual. I've seen a lot of northern lights hanging in the north or off to the west but never one that came right across the top of the sky."

Amazed, Lott called over his neighbor Larry Templeton.

"Larry thought it was pretty amazing too. I had my scope set up and we were looking at things for a while. After he went to bed...that's when this thing appeared to me. The angel."

The Angel

In Terry Lott's stargazing journal there is an entry that reads, "May 3, 1998. 11:30 p.m. Head, wings, robe." The entry is brief because at the time Lott was too excited to properly record what he'd seen.

"I was blown away," he remembers. "I think I was even on my knees praying."

The event that sparked such reverence was the sudden appearance of a being in the cloudy band overhead.

"All of a sudden," he says, "right in the middle, right above my head, that band turned into an angel. I'm telling you—a biblical angel, with the wings, the long cloak to the floor, and arms reaching out into the band. It had a head shape, shoulder shape, and it was right there in the middle of that beam. It was enormous."

From Lott's perspective, the angel appeared to occupy roughly one foot of sky, which could potentially make it hundreds of feet tall.

Unlike the nebulous band, through which he could see stars, Lott says the angel was opaque and blocked out everything behind it. He was so awestruck by the sight that he lost track of time.

"It felt like I'd been there in my front yard watching it for a long time, but I don't know," he says. "Gradually, it just dissipated, but for a while there it was just as real as real could be."

Though certain of his vision, Lott is ambivalent as to whether it was a religious experience in the classical sense.

"I'm kind of a spiritual guy," he says. "I do a lot of meditation when I go stargazing, so maybe I somehow conjured that. I mean... to see an absolute shape of an angel, maybe that's because of my belief in them or maybe it's one of those subjective things."

Whatever the case, Lott is unlikely ever to forget that night in May.

"I'm tellin' you... that just floored me."

CHAPTER 23

Just a Dream

The debate still rages as to whether the fringes of sleep are a playground for subconscious projections into the waking mind, a hole in the fabric of our awareness through which messages can slip from another plane of existence, or some amalgam of the two. My money is on the third option. Thanks to Beckie Campbell for giving me the interview that led to this and other chapters, and to Mike Cyronek for arranging it.

Hypnopompic and hypnagogic hallucinations—events witnessed while in the transition from a sleeping state to a waking one and vice versa—are a common explanation for paranormal experiences that occur in those states, and consequently such experiences are often thusly written off.

Beckie Campbell's childhood brush with the unknown was one such experience, though even some twenty-five years later she is not entirely convinced it was, as her mother said, "just a dream."

White Noise

When Beckie was a child, her family lived on Nichol Road, in the part of Revelstoke known as Arrow Heights. She says neither the home, an unassuming two-story built by her parents, Bill and Stacy, nor the land around it have any known history of paranormal activity, which makes her memory of white noise even harder to explain.

"I probably would have been six or seven years old," she recalls. "I remember waking up because I didn't feel well. You know how when you're a kid and you're sick, the first thing you do is call your mom? Well, that was the first thing I tried to do."

Sitting up, Beckie observed that her entire room was filled with what appeared to be electrical static.

"The whole room looked like I was stuck inside a snowy television—like there was white noise everywhere, but with no sound. I could barely see anything inside the room ... it was all fuzzy."

Outside the room, however, Beckie could see quite clearly, and she was confused by what she saw.

"I looked out my bedroom door and there were these glowing orbs going down the hall."

She describes the orbs as being "huge, a good two feet across, filling up pretty much the whole hallway."

"There was a line of them going down the hall," Beckie remembers. "That part of the hallway dead-ends in a wall, and I remember thinking they must somehow be going through it. I tried to call my mom but nothing would come out. I don't know if it was because I was scared or what."

One of the orbs passed directly by her bedroom door.

"After that, I was freaked right out. Another one was coming and I didn't want to deal with it, so I lay back down and tried to go to sleep. I didn't know what else to do."

The first thing Beckie did the next morning was tell her mother what had happened.

"My mother said it was just a dream, because how else do you explain it?" she says. "Now that I'm a mother, I think I understand—she didn't know what else to say."

Like so many people who have fleeting experiences such as these, when she looks back on that night, Beckie is still unable to fully make sense of what she saw.

"You don't think about it often, and when you do you kind of assume you had to be dreaming, but … it was so real. I physically remember waking up and not feeling well, trying to sit up and call my mom—all of it."

CHAPTER 24
Shadow People and Gremlins

At first, stories of gremlins were a bridge too far, even for someone writing a book about the supernatural. Eventually, when I kept running across stories, differing only in the names and locations involved, of tiny Shadow People causing electrical and mechanical problems, I relented. Strangely, despite their being common in paranormal literature, not one person from Revelstoke came forward to talk about encounters with full-on Shadow People; the only two interactions I was able to document were my own. Detailed in Chapter 17, "My Mother's House," they were the most frightening and inexplicable phenomenon I have ever witnessed.

Should any Revelstoke residents have encounters of their own they'd like to share, I would be very interested in hearing them.

Sightings of Shadow People are among the world's most commonly reported supernatural phenomena. Most often described as being the size of an adult human and completely black in color, with no definable features, reports differ on how Shadow People move—some observers say their movements are disjointed, others fluid—but most agree they move quickly, from shadow to shadow.

Their appearances tend to hold to a pattern: at first they are glimpsed from the corner of your eye, a dark flash that is gone by the time you look directly at it, leaving you only with a sense of unease. Over time the unease increases, along with the frequency of the flashes, until finally you see an apparition directly in front of you. They have been seen standing, running, at nighttime, and during the day. Those who have touched Shadow People report a feeling like electrical current running through their bodies. A few have described their meeting with Shadow People as marking the start of periods of great depression in their lives.

Less commonly reported are stories of small Shadow People who seem to be more irritating than frightening. The arrival of these creatures—often referred to by those who suffer them as "gremlins"—heralds any number of annoyances, from electrical malfunctions to mechanical failures, and while Shadow People appear to be tied to particular places, gremlins seem to be attached to people; in at least two of the stories described here, the creatures are said to have followed a person or persons to new locations.

"I guess we got Mom's gremlins"

Over the course of her life, Mary Dean has seen ghosts, viewed strange lights in the sky, and dreamed of events before they happened, but even she rejected the notion of little Shadow People, or gremlins—at least at first. Once they moved into her home, however, she began to reconsider, and once someone showed her a working method for deterring them, she became a believer.

Mary's husband, Chris, was estranged from his birth family for most of his adult life, and it wasn't until middle age that he was finally able to make contact with his birth mother, Janine. Janine, now elderly and living in Lethbridge, Alberta, was thrilled to hear from Chris and wished to meet him. So before long, he and Mary made the eight-hour trip east. Once there, he and Janine began the process of getting to know one another and the three became close, with Mary and Chris visiting whenever the opportunity presented itself. This is when Janine began to talk about her gremlins.

Mary remembers that Janine would experience electrical problems around her home: the lights would flicker, the television would cut in and out, sometimes even her car would conk out for no apparent reason, and Janine would always attribute the trouble to gremlins. Then, on the way home from what would be their last visit before Janine passed on, Chris and Mary began having problems with their truck.

These problems persisted after returning to Revelstoke, and soon they began having minor electrical problems in their home as well.

"It was little weird things," says Mary. "The lights would flicker on and off, but there'd be no major problems."

The two blamed the issues on old wiring in their home, although from time to time Chris would tease Mary by saying, "I guess we got Mom's gremlins."

"We made a joke of it," she remembers.

It stayed a joke until the day Mary let a co-worker in on it and got an unexpected reply.

"I was talking to this woman. Her family was from Ireland," remembers Mary. "I made a joke about [having gremlins], and she says, 'Do you know how to get rid of them? Give them an offering—a saucer of milk out by the main door that you use in your house."

Mary's first thought was that a saucer of milk by her front door would be good for endearing her to the neighborhood cats and not much else, but as the annoyances at her home escalated, she decided to try the woman's advice: she placed a bowl of milk outside the door to her house.

"We have two cats that live in the carport, and we used to get strays coming in to steal cat food," says Mary. "That milk sat there for three days … it was never touched."

The electrical disturbances stopped soon after.

Years later, Mary's daughter Carla began to have similar problems when she and her boyfriend moved into a new home in Catherwood Mobile Home Park, a remote area past the Revelstoke airport: her car would break down, they would have it repaired, and then his would do the same. This went back and forth for almost a month before Carla told her mom who, without hesitation, replied, "You've got gremlins. Put some milk out by your door."

While the girl was used to hearing strange things from her mother, this was an entirely new level, and it took some convincing on Mary's part before her daughter would try the experiment.

Says Mary: "She put out a saucer of milk … on her porch. She's out in the middle of nowhere, any animal can come and drink it, and [the milk] sat there for a couple of days, not touched."

After three days, Carla took the saucer back inside and her car troubles ceased.

"I've had gremlins for years—
I just figured you can't get rid of them"

As far as belief in the supernatural goes, Roma Sutherland is Mary Dean's diametric opposite: she has never seen a ghost, viewed an unexplainable light in the sky, or, until her experience with gremlins, encountered any phenomenon you might class as supernatural. As such, it never occurred to her that the electrical problems she experienced after moving into a new home with her boyfriend, Andrew, starting with a faulty porch light, were anything other than bad wiring and worse luck.

"It was really weird," she recalls. "At first the lights on the porch weren't working ... then all of a sudden the plugins where the TV was and then my microwave and computer."

After several electricians had come and gone without finding the source of the malfunctions, Sutherland was stuck for answers the day she complained about the problem to her friend Nancy.

"So each new phase is one step away from where your porch is?" Nancy asked.

Sutherland realized that was in fact the case and told her so.

"Go put milk out by your front door," said Nancy. "You've got gremlins."

It was the first time Sutherland had ever laughed in a friend's face.

"No, I don't."

Nancy was firm. "Yes, you do," she said. "They obviously moved in with one of you. Try it. You'll see."

The friends left it at that, but Sutherland's troubles soon wore her down and she placed a saucer of milk outside the front door, just ahead of the faulty porch light. Not wanting Andrew to ask any questions, she hid the saucer behind a potted plant and waited; within a couple of days everything was back to normal. She still won't quite admit that what took place in her house happened because of small Shadow People, gremlins, or anything to that effect, but she won't deny it either.

Andrew was much less surprised by the chain of events. When she hesitantly told him what she had done, his answer caught her completely off-guard.

"Yeah, I've had gremlins around for years," he said. "I just figured you can't get rid of them."

CHAPTER 25

The Girl on Highway 23

While the story of the girl on Highway 23 concerns the section of highway south of Revelstoke, there have been accounts of a ghostly hitchhiker, this one male, on the northern section of the highway as well. Those stories date back to the mid-1970s and are more anecdotal than those below. To date, I have not found anyone who claims to have actually seen the male hitchhiker on 23 North; the story told in Chapter 26, "Eyes in the Fog," comes the closest. Though the girl on Highway 23 has not been seen for many years, the road still has a very peculiar feel to it, especially when driven at night.

Almost anyone who has sat around a campfire has heard stories of ghostly hitchhikers. Though the specifics of such tales change from teller to teller, the broad outline is almost always the same: late one night, a bored or altruistic driver sees a lone figure walking along a deserted strip of road and stops to offer him or her a ride. Before long the driver begins to suspect there is something unusual about their new companion and, in due course, is proven right.

The stories have been part of popular culture so long—some people consider the thirteenth-century story of St. Christopher, as told in the *Golden Legend*, the oldest such tale—they are often dismissed as fantasies that fulfill our need for the unusual in day-to-day life. What is forgotten in this dismissal is the simple fact that legends often contain fragments of truth. The story of the girl on Highway 23 is one such fragment.

"There was a young girl crying for help"

It was a warm summer evening in the 1970s when Joan Astra's foster children came running into the house looking for their mother.

"It had been a hot, hot day, and our kids were sleeping out on the porch," she remembers. "They came in and said they could hear somebody crying for help."

The Astras' farmhouse was several kilometers south of Revelstoke on Highway 23, a remote, wooded stretch of road that ends at the Shelter Bay ferry terminal on Upper Arrow Lake. At that time, the ferry service only ran into early evening, and by this point in the night there was little reason for anyone to be on the road.

Astra hurried outside and immediately heard a child's voice calling from the darkness beyond the treeline, in the direction of the highway.

"There was a young girl crying for help," says Astra. "She was saying, 'Help me, please, please, somebody help me.'"

Ushering her children back inside, she phoned the Royal Canadian Mounted Police (RCMP).

"The police came up right away, and there was nobody on the road at all," remembers Astra. "They went up and down the highway. They looked and looked but there was nobody."

Astra was almost ready to believe she and the children had imagined the entire episode until the next morning, when she related the story to neighbor Hank Winlaw, whose farm was several miles down the road. As it turned out, Winlaw had in fact seen someone on the road the previous night—a young girl, maybe ten or twelve years old, pushing a bicycle with a large basket at the front, up the road toward Astra's farm. The girl was crying, and Winlaw assumed it was because she had broken curfew and would be punished.

"I thought she was one of your kids," he told Astra.

Several years later, Cheryl Astra, Joan's daughter, was out riding her horse on a bright, moonlit night when she came upon a young girl sitting in the ditch by the side of the road. The child was wrapped in a blanket, Cheryl remembers, and asked her for the time.

Concerned for the child's safety, Cheryl came directly home and told her mother.

"I told Cheryl that a little girl shouldn't be sitting there alone," remembers Joan. "We went down there, but she was gone. I called out that the girl could come and stay with us but nobody came."

The pair waited there by the side of the road for some time before turning back. It was then, on the walk back to their farmhouse, a strange feeling came over Cheryl; her memory of meeting the little girl took on a sort of unreality.

"Cheryl told me it was almost like it wasn't real," said Joan. "Like she wasn't really . . . you know—not a real person sitting there."

This was to be the Astra family's last encounter with the girl on Highway 23 but not the last time she was seen.

The Blizzard

The final reported sighting of the mysterious girl comes from the winter of 1980. Brothers Harold and Al Leacock were driving southbound in a blizzard on Highway 23, not far from the ferry landing, when they passed a young girl walking in the same direction. Though they no longer recall exactly what she was wearing, the Leacock brothers remember it was not at all appropriate for the sub-zero conditions that day.

Harold quickly reversed until they came upon the girl again, still trudging determinedly through the blizzard. The brothers offered the child a lift to the ferry, which she refused on the grounds she was headed for Revelstoke. They tried explaining that not only was she going in the wrong direction but she was almost fifty kilometers out of town and, given the howling wind, unlikely to make it very much farther dressed the way she was. The girl simply kept walking.

The brothers hurried to Shelter Bay landing where they alerted B.C. Ferries personnel, who, in turn, alerted Revelstoke RCMP. Just as before, the police responded immediately and, just as before, no one was ever found.

The girl on Highway 23 had disappeared again.

CHAPTER 26

Eyes in the Fog

This is the only firsthand account I could find of strange happenings on Highway 23 North, and it came to me almost by accident. The man on whom Troy Ellard is based is the brother of a woman who provided a number of leads for this book, and when he bumped into us one night at coffee, I had no idea who he was. The woman introduced him, and he sat quietly for a while until he slowly, grudgingly told this story. He left the table shortly afterward, and his sister admitted to being shocked that her famously laconic brother had spoken at all, never mind told a story she herself had never heard.

While he had no problem with me adapting his experience, he requested I not include his real name or circumstances, requests I was happy to grant.

Troy Ellard is a tall, quiet man around sixty years of age who has spent most of his life living in a small mobile home just outside Revelstoke city limits. On the subject of the supernatural he is more or less agnostic.

"I've never seen a ghost floating across a room toward me," he says. "So I have a real hard time believing people who say they have, but who knows? I sure can't explain what happened to me, so maybe there is something out there."

The event Ellard refers to happened in the early morning hours of November 4, 1973, and, by his own admission, is not a story he shares often.

"My friends and I were cruising around town on a Saturday night. I had a dark green 1960 Thunderbird, and a whole bunch of us were piled in there. It's Revelstoke, so there wasn't much going on. We decided to drive out to the old car dump at Silver Tip Falls and see if we could cut mufflers off some old junkers … maybe make a couple bucks selling them."

Silver Tip Falls was a small waterfall north of Revelstoke on Highway 23. The road was moved up the mountain in the early 1980s before the construction of the Revelstoke Dam—an event that also flooded out Silver Tip Falls—but in 1973, the Big Bend Highway snaked along the heavily forested Columbia River Valley and, at 2 a.m. on an overcast fall night, was about as dark as a road can be.

"By the time we got out there, a fog had come down and we were having a hell of a time picking out cars, so we decided to come back another time," says Ellard. "It was around three in the morning when we headed back south to town."

The fog was so thick Ellard couldn't see much farther than the hood of his T-bird, but still he recalls driving the empty highway at a good clip.

"We were young and stupid and going too fast," he admits. "I saw two eyes ahead of us in the fog, and I slammed on my brakes, but it was too late."

Ellard remembers bracing for what he believed would be the body of a hitchhiker tumbling over the top of his car, but it never came.

"We were all freaking out," he remembers. "I got out of the car and walked around but couldn't find anyone. There was no dent in my hood or anything, but I knew I had seen those eyes. Nothing else—just two eyes in the fog."

It was then Ellard made the discovery that forever cemented in his mind the night of November 4, 1973: whoever—or whatever—the eyes had belonged to, they had saved the lives of everyone in the car; had the boys kept driving, Ellard's Thunderbird would have sailed off the edge of the road and plummeted forty feet into the river below.

"It doesn't make any sense to me," says Ellard. "I have a hard time believing in that stuff … but I know what I saw."

CHAPTER 27

Louie, You're Dead!

Originally I hadn't planned to include stories about people being "visited" by dead loved ones because I felt there was no way for the witness to be objective; after all, who among us doesn't have at least one departed friend or family member we'd dearly love to see again? Once I decided that the purpose of this book was to entertain rather than educate, Larry Nelles's account of a spectral visitor in the night was the first story I included. His practicality in the face of something completely beyond his experience has made me smile since the first time I heard the story back in 2012.

Aside from a second-hand encounter with a UFO in the Arrow Lakes region, Larry Nelles has had limited experience with the supernatural. In fact, Nelles, an accomplished horseman known in equine circles as a quiet, practical man, has had only one such experience, and as far as he's concerned, it was enough to last a lifetime.

"My ex-wife's father, Louis Bafaro, died on August 3, 1978," Nelles recalls. "They found out he had cancer, sent him home, and the next day he passed away, back at the hospital. He was in a lot of pain."

At the time, Nelles was operating a bed-and-breakfast/horse ranch on a large parcel of land along Highway 23, south of Revelstoke. "Nelles' Ranch," as it was called, offered trail rides, riding lessons, and a Sunday brunch that was as popular with locals as it was with tourists. It was here that Nelles would have the visit that permanently changed the way he looked at the world.

The master bedroom in Nelles' Ranch was on the second floor. In order to get there, you passed through a small kitchen, which was used by the Nelles family as a quiet spot to have a moment away from guests. Nelles says it consisted of a small table with fold-out chairs, big enough to fit two or three people having coffee.

One night, some thirty days after the passing of his father-in-law, Nelles woke to find the kitchen light on.

"It would have been in the wee hours of the morning," he recalls. "Probably one or two o'clock, something like that."

Assuming he had forgotten to turn off the light before falling asleep, Nelles rose from bed and sleepily walked into the kitchen, where, sitting at the table in front of him, was none other than the recently deceased Louis Bafaro.

Says Nelles, "When I walked in, he was sitting in the chair on the far side of the table. I couldn't believe it. His hair was combed back and he had his glasses on. I froze."

The dumbstruck Nelles quickly found his composure.

"I said, 'Louie, you're dead. What are you doing here?' And he said to me, 'I had to come back and tell you to tell everyone that I'm okay. I'm not in any pain and everything is fine.'"

"How can this be?" Nelles asked.

"Look," said the spirit. "I just want you to let everybody know I'm okay and everything is fine."

"I told him I didn't believe this," says Nelles. "But that was it—the light was out and he was gone."

Nelles still struggles with how to quantify his experience. He says it was too vivid to be a dream, and the fact that he was still in the kitchen after it happened supports the idea that he was awake.

"I'd say a ghost is probably the nearest thing to describing it," he explains. "But I couldn't believe he was sitting there talking to me normally. That's the only experience I've ever had of speaking to someone who has passed away. I was afraid to mention it for a while, but eventually I told people about it. I was astounded—how can that happen?"

CHAPTER 28

Strange Tales of the Arrow Lakes

Though there are only five confirmed stories from the Arrow Lakes region presented here, I know for a fact there are more still out there. Many of them have come to me, albeit in fragments too small to be turned into stories, from friends and family of people who once lived in the valley's now-submerged townships. "Fear on the South Road" is adapted from the anonymous account "Strange Memories of Revelstoke" as first published by researcher Brian Vike of The Vike Factor *(www.the-v-factor-paranormal.blogspot. ca). Though he no longer tracks UFO sightings, Vike is still hard at work online, promoting his hometown of Houston, BC, with the blog* Houston, British Columbia *(www.houston-british-columbia-canada.blogspot.ca).*

The current residents of the home in "Just around the Bend" declined to be interviewed and asked that their property not be specifically identified. I agreed to this out of respect for their young children, who find the subject of the supernatural frightening and who have already gone through a period of excitement and fear following the episode described below.

As such, all names in this story have been changed along with some dates.

Regardless of your thoughts on the paranormal, the Arrow Lakes region is truly beautiful and worth visiting.

The 230-kilometer section of the Columbia River known as the Arrow Lakes stretches from Revelstoke Dam just north of town down to Castlegar in the south. Once two separate lakes, called Upper and Lower Arrow, Arrow Lake is now one continuous body of water steeply bordered by the Monashee Mountains to the west and Selkirk Mountains to the east. The two lakes joined when damming began on the Columbia River in the 1960s.

The area is quiet, its roads—Highways 6, 23, and 31—not heavily trafficked and the few towns that dot the region—Nakusp, Silverton, New Denver, Kaslo, and Trout Lake, to name a few—are all sparsely populated, the largest of them boasting only 1,500 residents. Once upon a time, however, the Arrow Lakes region had a thriving mineral economy and many more towns, including Ferguson, Sandon, Cody, Circle City, and Gerrard, sprang up to house the influx of miners.

Those towns have since faded into history, but their remains are seeded among the area's lush woodland and, should one look hard enough, can still be found on unnamed back roads.

Given all this, it is perhaps no surprise the Arrow Lakes region is a place of both beauty and mystery from which more than a few strange stories have emerged.

Fear on the South Road

The trip south of Revelstoke on Airport Way is a lovely, fourteen-kilometer drive that begins after the Illecillewaet River

Bridge, winds up through the wooded suburb of Arrow Heights, down the steep decline known as Red Devil Hill, and ends, with the pavement, where the Akolkolex Forest Service Road begins. It is a quiet, remote road that, before the Columbia River was dammed, led to the Arrow Lakes community of Arrowhead. The damming of the Columbia flooded some two-thirds of the Columbia River Valley's arable land, forcing communities such as Arrowhead, Beaton, and Burton to relocate and, in some cases, simply evacuate.

Even the area directly south of Revelstoke, past its modest airport, was once home to a number of thriving farms, which were abandoned when the reservoir began to fill. When the river is low enough, drivers on Airport Way can still make out the old highway beneath the water, snaking past the stone foundations of sunken homesteads.

It was here on Airport Way about forty years ago that one family out for an evening drive went through an unexplainable feeling of collective terror that baffles them to this day.

"The purpose of the trip was to find roads we'd not yet traveled"

It was the summer of 1975 when the Scott family of Nanaimo, B.C.—parents Paul and Lily, daughter Paige, and granddaughter Emily—decided to take a break from their lengthy road trip and stop in Revelstoke for the night.

"We were slowly traveling across British Columbia and planning to circle through part of Alberta before heading home," Paige recalls. "We arrived in Revelstoke late on a sunny summer afternoon, found a motel, and went for dinner."

After dinner, the Scotts took a walk through Revelstoke's compact downtown and afterward found themselves wanting to explore further.

On their map, the family saw Airport Way and the Akolkolex Forest Service Road threading down the east side of the Columbia River.

"The purpose of the trip was to try to find roads we'd not yet traveled," says Paige. "So … off we went."

The weather had been kind to the Scotts all day, but looking out over the river from the top of Red Devil Hill they could see they were leaving clear skies behind and heading straight into cloud cover; in the distance sheet lightning flashed. They had seen few cars on the road up to that point, but after Red Devil Hill, the Scotts didn't see another soul until they turned back.

Some four kilometers later, between the turnoffs for what are now Lenard Drive and Catherwood Road, a strange feeling came over Paige, who was sitting in the backseat with Emily.

"The road turned a sharp corner to the left and followed the base of the mountains around a large bay," she remembers. "The moment we turned the corner I was terrified … I wanted so much to ask my father to turn back."

Paige couldn't explain the feeling that had come over her.

"The logical side of me kept saying to not be silly," she remembers. "The purpose of the trip was to explore!"

Nevertheless, she found herself so terrified she could no longer look out the windows of the car. She began to play with Emily, who seemed blissfully unaware of her mother's escalating fear.

Suddenly, at a point roughly halfway around the bay, Paul pulled a hasty U-turn and sped back in the direction from which they'd come. He never spoke, but Paige heard her mother say quietly, "So you felt it too."

As soon as they had rounded that wide corner, the sun peeked through the clouds and the family's collective feeling of terror vanished. As they drove back toward Revelstoke, the only words spoken were by Paul.

"Promise me," he said, "that none of you will ever drive down that road again."

On the way back to the hotel, the Scott family didn't speak a word to each other about what had happened, which Paige says was completely out of character.

"Not only would we normally have talked about something like that," she says. "We would have driven back the next day to at least the beginning of the bay."

In fact, it was four years before the family broached the subject again. None of them could recall a single reason why they had been afraid—certainly they didn't remember seeing anything—but both Paul and Lily admitted to feeling the same sense of inexplicable, overwhelming terror that Paige had. The only member of the Scott family unaffected by the incident, whether because at two years old she was too young to understand or too small to see out the window, was Emily.

In addition to an almost paralyzing fear, Paul recalled being filled with the baffling certainty that "if we had kept going, we would have never come back." Even more bizarrely, each of the family members found that they had wanted to discuss the event at some point in the preceding four years but couldn't.

"I recall often trying to think about it and say something, but the thoughts and words just dissolved," recalls Paige. "That was happening with my parents as well. We still have no understanding or memory about what frightened us."

Some twenty years later, Paige returned to Revelstoke and the south road with her husband.

"Everything had changed with the lowering of the lake level and the growth of the trees," she recalls. "There was nothing at all frightening about the place."

Even so, she honored the promise she'd made to her father and declined to go past the corner where it had all began. The fear is gone, but forty years later Paige's memory still fragments when she tries to remember what happened to make her family feel what they did.

"I've stayed in Revelstoke many times since then but ... will never travel that road," she says. "Maybe someday I will remember why."

Pennsylvania

In late 2014, an experience similar to that of the Scott family, albeit with a shocking twist, was reported as having taken place in the woods of eastern Pennsylvania. The story goes that a man, while out walking his dogs on a remote, wooded road, found himself having to restrain the animals when they began barking madly at the trees on the left side of the road. Shortly after the dogs' mania began, a figure walked out of the brush some twenty feet ahead of them—a squat, muscled, hairy Sasquatch-type creature, albeit with a long, dog-like snout instead of the blunt, ape-like features with which such creatures are normally identified.

The animal strode across the road, never once giving any indication it was aware of the man or his barking dogs, finally disappearing into the brush on the other side. The shaken witness dragged his pets back to his car and fled, returning later in the day with several armed friends. The men began searching the forest where the animal disappeared, only to be stopped a short distance into the brush by an inexplicable feeling of shared dread. The group of well-armed men was stopped as one by the unshakeable feeling that to go any farther would mean their death. They turned back.

Just around the Bend

Not far from the wide, sweeping curve on Airport Way where the Scotts began to feel that inexplicable sense of dread, there sits a house where at least two families have had inexplicable experiences all their own. The home, a relatively new one by Revelstoke standards, looks nothing like your stereotypical haunted house, and yet when the Pike family moved in some fifteen years ago it wasn't long before they began to suspect something supernatural was happening around them.

Fast Steps in the Dark

At first, Lisa Pike thought she was dreaming the sound of footsteps.

"I'd hear the sound of people going up and down the stairs all the time," she remembers. "I'd wake up, get out of bed... I'd think it'd be our cat, but the cat was outside, the kids were sound asleep in bed. Sometimes this would go on all night long."

Realizing she wasn't dreaming the footsteps, Pike then pinned the noise on an overactive imagination. This didn't last long as her two daughters, Tanya and Kelly, soon began to hear the footfall as well; the pair told their mother about hearing "fast, springy steps" up the staircase.

Curiously, Pike's husband, Steven, never heard the noises nor did he experience any of what followed.

"My husband doesn't believe in this sort of thing," she explains. "He thought we were being silly, that it was all explainable, but too many weird things happened to ignore."

One such weird thing occurred during a sleepover birthday party for Tanya, the elder daughter.

"This was when my daughter was twelve or thirteen years old," Pike remembers. "In the morning, the kids asked me what had been going on with the cat last night. They said they heard it running up and down the stairs and going crazy."

Pike was nonplussed.

"The cat was outside," she said. "I just let him in this morning."

Escalation

As with many hauntings, it wasn't long before the presence in the Pike family home manifested itself in a more direct way. Lisa remembers:

"In our kitchen there's a six-cupboard pantry. One morning I got up—the kids were still in bed, my husband had gone to work—and I came around the corner into the kitchen and all the cupboard doors were open on the pantry. I thought my husband was playing a joke on me or something, right? Thinking I'd walk into these doors. Except when he got home, he swore to me he didn't do it."

After the incident involving the pantry doors, Pike began noticing that a set of venetian blinds in one of the upstairs windows had taken on a mind of its own.

"I opened my blinds one morning," she says. "Then later we were outside—and I happened to look up at the window and the blinds were closed. I asked the kids who had closed them, and they all claimed they hadn't. I went in and opened the blinds then went back outside. A couple of hours later, I looked and the blinds were closed. That happened several times."

Another unusual event occurred while Steven was away on business.

"The girls were quite little and would sleep downstairs with me [when Steven was out of town]," says Pike. "This one time, I woke up and the girls were still asleep, so I went upstairs to collect laundry and saw the sheets had been pulled back on one of the beds. No one had been upstairs and yet somebody had been in my daughter's bed."

Worried an intruder had somehow gained access to the house, Pike checked all the doors and windows but found everything secure. Making the possibility of an intruder even more improbable was the fact that nothing else had been disturbed.

"You know what?" says Pike. "Some of this stuff can be explained away, I guess. Lots of people would dismiss it but this wasn't explainable."

The Little Girl in the Blue Dress

The Pikes experienced other strange things over the course of their time in the house around the bend—some nights Tanya would awake in her upstairs bedroom to see, in light cast by the family computer outside her door, their office chair spinning by itself—but only one phenomenon would be observed by anyone outside the Pike family. This was the little girl in the blue dress.

Lisa remembers a lazy summer afternoon when Kelly was five years old. Steven was out of town on business and the Pike women were in the backyard enjoying the afternoon sun when Kelly casually mentioned playing with her "new friend." Lisa, unaware of any new kids having moved into the neighborhood, asked Kelly where she had met her new friend and was not at all prepared for her daughter's nonchalant reply:

"She lives with us."

"She swore by that for years," says Lisa. "She still says, 'Yes, there was a little girl and she wore a long blue dress and had long black hair.'"

Nonetheless, the Pikes were not disturbed by the phantom, and aside from Kelly's infrequent mentions of the spectral child, she was all but forgotten. That changed years later when the Pikes, who had long since moved to a new home, received a phone call from a woman whose daughters had been babysitting for the latest residents of the house around the bend.

According to the woman, her daughters had been looking after the couple's young children, a boy and a girl, and noticed the girl often referred to her "sister."

"They told her that she didn't have a sister," says Lisa. "She said, 'Yes I do. She comes and stays with me every night and leaves really early in the morning. Then she goes to the bushes.'"

Lisa asked the caller if the child had described her "sister." Says Lisa:

"The little girl describes her as having long dark hair and a long blue dress."

"Strange Object Seen in South Heavens"

Beneath the surface of the Upper Arrow some twenty-five miles south of Revelstoke lies the remains of Sidmouth, one of many small communities flooded in 1968 when the much-contested Hugh Keenleyside Dam was built on the Columbia River, five miles upstream of Castlegar. Like residents of other flooded communities, the people of Sidmouth were given little say in the decision that saw their homes relocated and their town become part of the Arrow Lakes Reservoir.

Almost fifty years later, the little bit of Sidmouth not covered by water is an overgrown tangle of fir, spruce, and alder trees accessible only by boat or helicopter. It is a quiet, contemplative place that gives no indication it was the site of Revelstoke's first reported instance of strange lights in the sky. Many more would follow, but that fall night in 1950 was the most widely observed and reported until the Revelstoke meteor impact of 1965.

On the night of October 15, 1950, H. Eynsbergen (no first name was ever given), engineer in charge of the Pacific Asbestos Corporation's mine site, and seven of his crew spied an object in the night sky. According to a report in the October 19, 1950, edition of the *Revelstoke Review* under the headline "Strange Object Seen in South Heavens," what Eynsbergen and his men saw was a "strange, oval-shaped object with a bluish white light." Using binoculars, the engineer was able to get a better view of the object, which, according to the article, resembled a "huge light globe swinging to and fro" and was estimated to be some 30,000 feet up.

Eynsbergen and his men go on to say that the object remained in the sky above the Monashee Mountains for thirty minutes, from 9:30 to 10 p.m., before disappearing to the southeast.

The incident was also reported in the October 18, 1950, edition of the *Vancouver Sun* under the headline, "Maybe Another Flying Saucer?"

Strange Music

Comaplix was once a vibrant sawmill town on the north shore of the Arrow Lakes offshoot known as Beaton Arm, and like most of the towns in the region there is very little physical evidence to mark its existence today. Unlike other towns in the region, however, the disappearance of Comaplix had nothing to do with the flooding of the Arrow Valley. Instead, in 1915, Comaplix, along with the steamship S.S. *Revelstoke*, burned to the ground in a great fire, the origin of which has never been determined.

This is far from the only mystery the long-vanished town has to offer. Three years before the fire, in 1912, local prostitute Fanny St. Clair was found brutally murdered in her home; according to the Nelson newspaper the *Nelson Daily News*, "She had been cut across the face and head with a beer bottle and one large piece of glass was imbedded in her skull so deeply that it was difficult to remove it. She had also been struck twice with a hammer." Her killer was never found.

Almost a century later, a group of men camping by the lakeshore would discover that even though Comaplix is gone, its mysteries remain.

"Did you hear that?"

One summer night in 2005, Greg Valance and his two brothers were camping in the area, intending to explore with their metal detectors.

"We were camped at the end of the road ... right by the creek. Our fire was overlooking the lake, our tents were about 150 feet behind us," he said. "It was dark, probably ten at night."

As the men sat around the campfire, they noticed their dogs, which had previously been lying at their feet, begin to fidget.

"We had four dogs, and for no reason their ears went up and they started looking around," says Valance. "Then they looked toward where our tents were set up ... and started growling."

Following their dogs' gaze toward the treeline, Valance and his brothers expected to see a bear trundling out of the dark but instead saw only their tents and the shadows beyond. Instead of a bear, the darkness produced something completely different—the sound of a piano.

"We looked at each other and said, 'Did you hear that?'" remembers Valance. "All three of us heard it at the same time. It was as clear as anything. Like somebody playing the piano—not a complete song, but a few notes."

The sound faded almost as quickly as it had come, leaving the three brothers mystified. They tried to produce a rational explanation, but the remote location of their campsite made it difficult.

"We were camped on a dead-end road. The main dirt road was way above us, and we took a switchback down to the lake," he said. "The sound was clear, like it was right there—there's no way it could have carried across the lake from Beaton. And we weren't drinking, we weren't smoking drugs."

The brothers stayed at the campsite for several days afterward, but that was their only experience with the strange music. Eight years later, Valance still has no explanation, but the experience prompted him to learn more about the long-lost town of Comaplix. He was not particularly surprised by what he found.

"There's a book called *Silent Shores and Sunken Ships*, published by the Arrow Lakes Historical Society," says Valance. "In there it says, 'When the lights go down, when the lights go out, it's time to leave Comaplix.' Like strange stuff is happening there."

He laughs.

"I know that for sure."

The Light on the Lake

It was the summer of 1977 when three crew members aboard a B.C. Ferries vessel saw a strange object flying low in the night sky above the Arrow Lakes. At the time, Larry Nelles was a ship's mate aboard the ferry, which ran passengers between Shelter and Galena Bay in the Upper Arrow. Though Nelles didn't see the object himself, he remembers the vessel had just made its final trip of the night and was heading for home when his shipmates burst in on him in the ship's office.

"It was a clear, blue night," remembers Nelles. "There was Henry Nelson, John Twibill, and Malcolm Woods . . . they come running in the office . . . they were astounded."

The three men excitedly told Nelles they had just seen a black object the size of a football field traverse the night sky some hundred feet above the ship.

"They said that there were blue flames coming out the back, and it was silent," says Nelles. "The thing was going very slow, and then all of a sudden it left and there was just a blue streak in the sky—it was gone."

Nelson, the ship's oiler, sketched what they had seen. Nelles says the drawing bore some resemblance to a dirigible, at least in shape. If the men's stories are to be believed, however, the object moved much faster than any airship, and Nelles had no reason to question their credibility.

"Henry Nelson was the kind of guy who wouldn't admit to something unless it was true ... it's just the way he was," says Nelles. "And John Twibill—he was the ship's engineer—he didn't believe in UFOs. But when he saw this, he believed."

After the initial excitement wore off, the men found themselves unsure not only of what they'd seen but whether or not they should tell anyone else.

"They were all a little mystified by it," says Nelles. "So consequently they didn't really tell anyone else. People think you're seeing things, so you're afraid to say too much."

What the three men thought of the object, or whether they ever saw it again, we can only guess. Each died from natural causes within a sixteen-month span six years later—the fifty-four-year-old Twibill first on April 18, 1982; Nelson, sixty-three, on April 2, 1983; and finally Malcolm Woods, age fifty, on August 18 of the same year.

Though Nelles, who lived for decades in the area south of Revelstoke before relocating to rural Arizona, had never heard of anything like it before and hasn't since, this is hardly the first time an unidentified flying object producing blue flame has been seen.

On the morning of January 12, 1910, residents of Chattanooga, Tennessee, rushed outside in the thousands to see what appeared to be a white, cigar-shaped object traveling the sky above their city. As reported by newscaster Frank Edwards in his 1966 book *Flying Saucers, Serious Business*, the object was in plain view and had "a line of flickering blue flames which played along the undersides of the craft for almost its full length." According to witnesses, after circling the city a number of times, the object slowly moved off over the mountains and out of sight; perhaps not coincidentally, fifteen minutes later a similar object was sighted over Huntsville, Alabama, some seventy-five miles away.

The same volume tells of Socorro, New Mexico, police sergeant Lonnie Zamorra, who, while on patrol on April 24, 1964, observed a shining object drift across the afternoon sky. He pursued the object well beyond the town limits, at which point he heard what sounded like an enormous explosion. Zamorra eventually found the object in a gully, where he discovered it was egg-shaped, between twelve and fifteen feet in length, and, at that moment, being examined by two small figures "in white or silvery coverall type garments." As soon as the individuals in the gully noticed Zamorra watching them, all parties panicked, and as he ran for his car, Zamorra heard another great explosion, this one followed by a jet of flame from the bottom of the now-rising craft. That flame was blue.

While we can't say exactly what happened in any of these cases, it is clear the paranormal events noticed in the Arrow Lakes region are not unique to the surrounding area, but rather part of a much farther-ranging experience, the true nature of which we can only guess.

CHAPTER 29

The Angel and the UFO

I stumbled on the story of Harold Howery quite by chance while doing general research. I was fortunate enough, with a little help from the Howery family in Alberta, to locate his wife, Frieda, whose memory of the event proved invaluable. During the course of writing this book, I read some forty volumes on various facets of the paranormal, and this was the only mention of Revelstoke I could find. Online it's a different story. There are more accounts of paranormal activity—usually of the UFO or Sasquatch variety—being published all the time, though none in quite so much detail as provided by the Howerys and John Keel.

While much of Revelstoke's paranormal history has never been formally recorded, indeed most of it has never made it past city limits, the town nevertheless once managed to attract the attention of famed paranormal researcher John Keel.

Keel, an American author and researcher best known for *The Mothman Prophecies*, a chronicle of his involvement with Point Pleasant, West Virginia's infamous 1966 to 1967 wave of paranormal activity, also wrote heavily on the subject of UFOs.

In books such as *Our Haunted Planet, Strange Creatures from Time and Space,* and *Operation Trojan Horse,* Kiel, who died in 2009, searched for patterns and similarities in UFO accounts from around the world, trying to draw from them an explanation as to what was being seen, and why.

In 1968 Keel's investigation expanded to encompass the Revelstoke area when he was contacted by a Hannah, Alberta, businessman named Harold Howery. From 1970's *Operation Trojan Horse:*

"[Howery] was driving west from the village of Revelstoke late at night when a circular object suddenly descended about 60 feet in front of his car, swaying from side to side like a pendulum. It was one large light, he said, of a light-blue shade. There was no noise and his car didn't stall. The object hovered for a few moments then flew off southward."

As described here, the light seen by Howery bears an uncanny resemblance to the blue light globe seen swinging some 20,000 feet in the sky by a group of miners in 1958, a story further detailed in Chapter 28, "Strange Tales of the Arrow Lakes."

Though Howery himself passed away in 2011, he is survived by his wife, Frieda, who was with him during the strange sighting in 1968 and whose recollection of events expands on Harold's account in some ways while contradicting it in others. In addition, her memory of a key event from Harold's youth again raises the question of a connection between so-called UFOs and other aspects of the supernatural.

Frieda

In the fall of 1968, Harold and Frieda Howery were traveling to Winfield, British Columbia, from their home in Hannah, Alberta, when the light appeared. Harold was forty-four years old.

Rather than the object appearing in the late night, as Harold told it, Frieda remembers it was "not dark yet, but not bright daylight, either." She also believes the sighting may have in fact occurred on the highway east of Revelstoke, which would put them nearer, if not directly within, the paranormally active Rogers Pass area.

Frieda says the light was a bright white, circular object that looked "sort of like a cloud" roughly the size of their car. She remembers the unusual "cloud" appearing some six feet above their car, and pacing them no matter how fast they drove.

"I can remember Harold driving a bit faster, and then it moved faster. When he slowed down, it slowed down. Then it just disappeared."

This was not quite the end of the experience, however, as shortly before the cloud's disappearance, the Howerys observed another light approaching them in the oncoming lane.

"It was a light when we first saw it," remembers Frieda. "Then as it passed, we realized it was a car."

This would not be remarkable in and of itself, except that, according to Frieda, the car vanished.

"It just disappeared in our rearview mirror," she recalls. "For days we wondered what it meant, but then it kind of left our minds, I guess. We never talked about it again."

It Called Him by Name

Frieda says this was not the first time her husband had experienced something out of the ordinary. Harold had been a devout Christian, something Frieda says stood out about him and helped him make his way in the world.

"He was only seventeen when he joined up to the Air Force," she remembers. "They were all in this big building in Toronto, training, and he got the bottom bunk. Every day he would get down, pray, and read the Bible. Because of this he made friends who were Christians, who were all happy he had done that."

Harold's Christianity was a heartfelt commitment that lasted until the end of his life, and, as Frieda tells it, all began the day he saw the angel.

"Harold's family wasn't religious," remembers Frieda. "But later, thanks to Harold's influence, they became Christians too."

When Harold was a child, his family lived on farms, first near Okotoks, Alberta, and later near Spondin. It was while living in the Spondin area that Harold would have his encounter.

"When he was maybe five or six years old," says Frieda, "there was a gully … I guess where a lake or slough had been, but it was dry … He would go down there to play, and one day, while he was out playing, he heard someone call his name."

Harold turned at the sound, and saw, standing at the edge of the gully, a radiant white being, human in form, with enormous wings on its back.

"He couldn't remember a face, but he remembers it calling him by name," says Frieda.

The angel called Harold's name once more, then disappeared, leaving behind a stunned and newly devout Harold Howery.

The Question

After seeing the light outside Revelstoke, Harold and Frieda discussed the possibility of there being some connection to his childhood vision.

"I told him maybe it was another angel," remembers Frieda. "But there was really only a circular cloud shape. It didn't have anything else that we thought looked like an angel or anything."

Though there may not have been any direct similarities between the two events, it is curious that Harold was witness to both, and it raises the question of whether the experiences were related in another way. Is it possible that Harold Howery's experience as a child on the prairies outside of Spondin, Alberta, somehow changed him, opening him to further encounters if he chanced upon a place where they were already happening? Or perhaps whatever agency appeared to him in the gully on that day in 1930 was, for reasons only it can understand, checking up on him again some thirty-eight years later.

Far more likely is that the cause of and reasons for Harold's experiences will forever remain a mystery to us, at least until we pass across the same gulf as have he, and John Keel, and so many others before us.

CHAPTER 30

The Orange Triangle

Here we are again in UFO territory. James Bell's account was the first I'd heard of the Orange Triangle, but it wasn't long before I found another, an anonymous report submitted to the Alberta UFO Study Group, which became the story, "We figured it was just a trick with the trees." While these two stories are the only reported instances of the Orange Triangle in the Revelstoke area, the USA-based National UFO Reporting Centre has logged countless viewings of the phenomenon across North America since 2005. In fact, the phenomenon is so ubiquitous it has earned its own book: 2014's The Complete Story of the Worldwide Invasion of the Orange Orbs, *by Terry Ray.*

Interestingly, though Bell's memory of the incident remains fresh, his companion—who was willing to be interviewed but not identified—has found their recollection fading. Beckie Campbell's story is much the same, except her companions have no memory of the incident at all. These experiences are remarkably similar to that of the Scott family in Chapter 28's "Fear on the South Road"; Olympe and Joan Astra's foster daughter in Chapter 25's "'There was a young girl crying for help"'; and my own, among others. It raises the question of whether the mind actively seeks to forget incidents that do not conform to expectations of reality or if there is some mysterious external factor disrupting the memories of some people who witness extraordinary events.

The story of Edna Tass and Rose Janiwicz is adapted from an anonymous account submitted to UFO*BC (www.ufobc.ca).

Finally, while I mention the presence of the Canadian military, it is because they are part of the stories as told to me. I do not believe the various intelligence apparatus of North American governments are participating in a cover-up of extraterrestrial contact. While there is likely to be extraterrestrial life somewhere out there (it's a big universe), I don't think they're here, darting around in the shadows and performing strange experiments.

White lights, blue sparks, and an indistinct brick-like object disappearing into a point of light—these are only a handful of the unusual phenomena observed in the skies above Revelstoke since 1950. Their strangeness aside, the only thing they have in common is an apparent uniqueness. That is, each phenomenon has been observed, or at least reported, only once. This uniformity makes the Orange Triangle even more of an anomaly than might ordinarily be considered.

The Orange Triangle is almost exactly that—a series of moving orange lights in a triangle formation that has been seen in the night sky above Revelstoke on at least two occasions, once in 2010 and again in 2011. Both times, witnesses reported seeing the lights well above the tops of nearby mountains, and both times, the sightings were followed by reports of a military presence, raising the question of whether the Orange Triangle is a manmade phenomenon or unusual enough that it has attracted the attention of Canada's Department of National Defence.

The experiences of the first witnesses to the Orange Triangle raise another question as well—are reports of strange lights in the sky also somehow linked to occurrences of supernatural activity?

"We figured it was just a trick with the trees"

On the night of March 2, 2010, friends Rose Janiwicz and Edna Tass were driving west toward Revelstoke on Highway 1 when they noticed what appeared to be a white light in the sky ahead of them.

"It was an oddly bright light flashing on and off quite high in the sky," says Tass, who was sitting in the passenger's seat. "We figured it was just a trick with the trees."

Not long after spying the light, Tass noticed a young girl standing by the side of the road ahead.

"I saw her clear as day," she remembers. "She had a pink winter jacket, black tight pants, a blonde ponytail, and a stare that creeped me right out."

It is this appearance that calls into question the link between strange events on the ground and in the sky, because when Tass pointed out the girl, who had been completely motionless, to Janiwicz, she vanished.

Tass adamantly rejects the idea that what she saw was a product of her imagination.

"I [first] saw a girl standing in the ditch out my peripheral vision," she says. "When I told [Rose] about her, she disappeared."

As is often the case with such inexplicable events, the two quickly put the disappearing girl out of their heads and focused on the flashing light above Revelstoke. Upon entering town, the two found a pullout area near the side of the road with an unobstructed view of the sky from which to observe the display.

"It was well above the mountains," remembers Tass. "But rather than being west of us like it was previously when we were coming toward the town, it was more south, as if it were hovering above the town."

The pair also observed that the light had increased in size.

After several minutes, the women left Revelstoke and continued their journey west, stopping again to watch the sky at a clearing not far out of town. By this point, the white light had become elongated, almost into an hourglass shape, and was joined by two other, more spherical, beacons.

"I saw the bright object with two orange lights with it now," says Tass. "One of them was above the white light and one below."

These new arrivals also flickered at seemingly random intervals.

The lights then changed formation, moving into a triangle shape, before the white light disappeared from view.

Getting back into the car, Tass and Janiwicz continued west for a few minutes more, until their curiosity demanded they make another stop. This time they pulled off the highway at a vantage point high above the tree line, with a clear view of the starless night sky.

Over the years, some who claim to have seen strange lights over Revelstoke have confused the headlamps of snowmobiles on the mountainside for something more mysterious, but Tass dismisses this explanation.

"They [the lights] were well above any mountaintops in the area," she says.

Janiwicz told Tass she had caught sight of a fourth light, again white, to the southwest of the elongated one shortly before it disappeared. Just as she was pointing out its location, the elongated light again appeared in the sky, this time almost double its previous size.

"While we were watching," says Tass, "the top orange light moved nearly instantaneously from its forty-five-degree position relative to the other one, to a position nearly straight above it."

The two women watched for some time afterward, noting that all four lights would flicker but only the white ones would disappear for any length of time. Stranger than everything they had observed was the feeling experienced by both as they witnessed the unusual lights.

"It felt like someone was pumping a hundred million volts through my body," recalls Tass. "It felt so strange and energizing that we both barely even noticed the next hour." She goes on to describe this positive buzz as lasting well into the next day, when they returned to Alberta.

It was on this return journey the two women claim to have seen numerous "military-looking" vehicles while passing back through Revelstoke, itself allegedly hemmed in by a thick fog that began one kilometer before town and ended one kilometer after, rising to a height of some 200 meters.

"There were no markings at all on them," says Tass. "But they were painted in the distinct military green."

The pair also claim to have seen what they described as a tractor-trailer pulling away equipment painted in the same style as the unmarked trucks. Tass recognized what she believed to be two enormous generators on the trailer, along with other, unrecognizable, hardware.

East of Revelstoke the pair claim to have been passed by three Chevy Tahoe SUVs, all with government-marked Alberta license plates. On the long drive home, both Janiwicz and Tass say they observed a number of such license plates on a variety of high-end automobiles, always traveling in groups of three. Their last sighting of these vehicles was on the section of Highway 2 between Airdrie and Innisfail, Alberta, in which they claim to have seen eighteen of the northbound Chevy Tahoe SUVs with similar license plates.

As the two women left the highway at Innisfail, we can only speculate as to where the government vehicles were headed, but the Canadian Forces base at Cold Lake, Alberta—some five hours north—seems a likely guess.

"Two days later we heard jets"

One evening in October 2011, two people—Revelstoke resident James Bell and a friend who asked not to be identified—were traveling east toward Revelstoke on Highway 1 when they spotted a series of strange lights in the night sky. The pair were four and a half kilometers west of town, near the Great White North Bar and Grill, when they observed a trio of bright circular orange lights arranged in what Bell described as an equilateral triangle above the peak of Mount Cartier.

Bell pulled his vehicle off the road to observe the phenomenon.

"It was about the size of the windshield," he remembers. "[The lights] sat there and didn't move, at least not at first."

A light rain on the roof of their SUV was the only sound as Bell and his friend watched the three orbs hanging motionless in the sky. Suddenly, the light at the bottom right of the triangle traveled upward—almost instantaneously—to join the light at the top, and all three lights blinked before disappearing. After the disappearance of the light, the pair sat stunned, trying to understand what they had just seen.

"We didn't really know what to think," says Bell. "Sometimes you see light coming off Cartier but it's just the headlamp on a snowmobile. This wasn't that—two of these lights were below the peak of the mountain, but the third was above it."

The two friends resolved to put the incident out of their minds and return to Revelstoke. Two days later, Bell was enjoying a cigarette outside his home when he heard the unmistakable sound of jets overhead, flying above the cloud cover.

"It was around 8:30 or 9 p.m. when I heard them," he remembers. "Sometimes at night you can hear the sound of jetliners flying, but these were three or four low-altitude passes by fighter planes."

Though the sound of jet fighters passing overhead isn't completely unheard of in the Revelstoke area, Bell believes the timing of this particular flight—coming as it did only two days after sighting the Orange Triangle—was no coincidence.

"What I think," says Bell, "is they were investigating whatever it was we saw."

The Military Angle

In both cases presented here, sightings of the Orange Triangle were followed by reports of a military presence in and around the Revelstoke area. Thinking there may be some connection between the two, I submitted a formal Access to Information request, asking for details of military movement in the Revelstoke area, to the Canadian Department of National Defence. Their response, including e-mails and flight logs, shows the Armed Forces were indeed in the Revelstoke area on March 2, 2010—to help the community commemorate the 1910 Rogers Pass Avalanche, which killed fifty-eight railroad workers. No mention was made of the jets heard by James Bell in October 2011 or of rogue lights in the sky.

Winter Lights

Beckie Campbell's experience with the Orange Triangle differs from the other two accounts in both its time frame—it occurred in the late 1990s—and lack of military presence. That's not to say there wasn't a military component, only that if it was present, she was unaware.

"It was winter 1996 or 1997," she recalls. "I would have been sixteen or seventeen. It was nighttime, maybe six or seven, and I was driving up Highway 23 North with my friends, going up to Viers Crescent to see another friend, when we saw lights on Boulder Mountain."

Beckie says the three orange, circular lights were well below the peak of the mountain, at least at first. Much like James Bell and his companion, the group initially ascribed to them a mundane explanation.

"It was winter, so at first we figured it was snowmobiles," she says. "That just made sense."

Also much like James Bell's story, this explanation lasted only a short time.

"Once we got closer to Viers Crescent," says Beckie, "the lights just weren't on the mountain any more. They were in the valley between Boulder and Frisby Ridge. Three of them, all in a horizontal line, hovering there. Not moving."

Arriving at their friend's house, the group got out of the car and continued observing the strange lights.

"We were standing in the yard, watching. Just then, the two on the side shot off away down the valley."

The remaining light then split into two and followed the others west. Afterward, Beckie and her friends went inside and tried to tell the others about what they'd seen.

"I remember sitting inside at their house," she says. "We were telling them about it and they told us we were crazy, that we didn't know what we were talking about, that we were high. I can guarantee you I wasn't doing drugs."

Undeterred, she kept her eyes on the basement window, scanning the small slice of sky in her view for another glimpse of the lights, which never again made an appearance.

Years later, Beckie is confident in her memory of the event but has no idea what it means or even exactly what it was that she saw. Her friends, however, do not remember the event.

"When I asked them about it a few years later, they didn't know what I was talking about," recalls Beckie. "I don't know if they forgot or what."

Of the lights she says:

"They didn't behave like any aircraft I have ever seen—especially the one that split in two. There was no movement—they were just there, and then they were gone. We have a lot of helicopters in the sky around here, but you hear them. These didn't make any sound at all ... and you know when a helicopter hovers, they usually move at least a little bit? These were static. I don't have a clue."

CHAPTER 31
Sasquatch

There is a considerably higher volume of Sasquatch sightings than can be found below; the owners of a number of online reports did not respond to my requests to adapt their material and so I was forced to exclude it. Those stories are worth seeking out, however, and a Google search of "Revelstoke" and "Sasquatch" should be enough to find what you're looking for. The first story presented here, "Footprints," is adapted from an account first reported on UFO*BC (www.ufobc.ca); the second, "'This was definitely not a bear,'" comes from one of my oldest friends, who asked to remain anonymous. The remainder are a collection of local lore, both old and new.

Debate about the existence of Sasquatch, the towering mountain ape said to exist in remote forests, has raged for decades and, barring the sudden discovery of a corpse or, even more unlikely, a colony of the beasts, the debate is likely to continue for decades to come. While popular arguments against the existence of Sasquatch most often center on the unlikelihood of such a sizable creature going undiscovered in our modern urban sprawl, or the lack of remains, one working theory answers such questions but, in doing so, introduces even larger mysteries into the world of Sasquatch.

A succinct description of this theory can be found in John Keel's 1975 book *The Eighth Tower: On Ultraterrestrials and the Superspectrum*, in a passage that refers to a number of legendary animals:

> Where does a dinosaur hide? Or a 90-foot sea serpent? Or an 18-foot-tall, hairy humanoid? Do they creep into a hidden network of deep caverns, as some of the believers claim? It is more probably that these are not actual animals but are distortions of our reality, inserted into our space-time continuum by ... mischievous forces ...
>
> Some of our funny monsters remain in an area for several days and are seen by many people before they finally disappear. Token attacks on domestic animals occur throughout the period, because the monster is somehow replenishing its diminishing energies with earthly animal matter. But it is a losing battle and the monster must ultimately melt away ...

While such a scenario would go some distance toward explaining the inconsistencies described above, it is, of course, not quite an answer unto itself; unanswered are pressing questions such as, "Who exactly are these mischievous forces?" Certainly, Keel had his theories, just as other researchers have had theirs, but there is as yet no definitive answer, and until there is, we are left to examine each instance where the creatures appear and draw our own conclusions.

Footprints

A seven-woman tree-planting crew was the first group of people on record to report anything Sasquatch-related in the Revelstoke area. The year was 1974, and the women were working on a short-term contract twenty-five kilometers southeast of Revelstoke, near the Akolkolex River in the Arrow Lakes region. Several days into the contract, the women began to feel uneasy—feeling as though they were being watched. Others in the group noted the area in which they were working had taken on an unpleasant smell, with no ready explanation as to why. Several days after this, tree planter Marie Spanza found two parallel sets of footprints, one smaller than the other, leading from a cliff farther up the mountain down to a nearby creek. The group decided not to explore the origins of the footprints and instead attempted to preserve them using cardboard boxes as cover. There is no further information as to whether the strange feelings the group experienced continued after this discovery or if the remainder of the tree-planting contract passed uneventfully.

"This was definitely not a bear"

It would be late October 2013 before another strange animal was sighted by the side of the road outside Revelstoke. Though he can no longer pin down the exact day, Chris Tate remembers it was around 5:30 in the morning when he came around a bend some sixty-five kilometers east of town and saw something unexpected in the tree line to his right.

"I was driving to work," he recalls. "I had my morning coffee with me, you know, and I came around the corner and saw something brown standing kind of in the ditch."

At first glance, Tate thought what he was seeing was a bear, and he slowed his speed accordingly.

"I was going pretty good," he says. "A hundred or 120 kilometers per hour or so, and I slammed on the brakes. Slowed right down because, I'm thinking, all I need to do is smoke a bear on the way to work. After that, I was doing maybe 30 to 40 kilometers per hour."

The reduced speed gave Tate more time to assess the creature, which he quickly realized was not a bear. First and foremost, the thing was standing on two legs rather than four.

"I've been around the bush out here a lot," he says. "I know bears. Even hit one with my truck on a different road in that area a month before … and sure, sometimes they stand up to scratch their backs on trees and stuff, but this was definitely not a bear."

In contrast to the towering behemoths described by other witnesses, the creature seen by Tate was short, between five and five and a half feet tall, covered in long hair he estimates was around six to eight inches long. Though he couldn't make out facial features, Tate remembers the creature had an oval head, closer in resemblance to that of a human than a bear. Another interesting difference from other reported sightings is that the creature did not appear to be thickly muscled.

"It had such long hair you couldn't really see muscles on it or anything," says Tate. "But it wasn't built like a bear—bears are bulky. It was more a human kind of build."

As he approached the part of the road nearest to where the small creature stood, it reached out a hand to a nearby birch tree, pivoted around it, and walked back into the tree line. The beast's seemingly dextrous use of its hands to turn around also struck Tate as being dissimilar from the habits of bears.

"Using his right hand, he grabbed the tree palm back ... like he twisted the wrist around to the front of the tree," says Tate. "He used it to pull himself forward around the front of the tree, then slowly walked into the bush. It was dusky out, still pretty dark, so once it went three feet into the bush I couldn't see anything. It's so thick in there, with all that small spruce, alder, you know ... even on a good, clear day you can't see more than ten feet ahead of you."

Once the creature vanished from sight, Tate resumed speed and drove to work, where he declined to share what he'd seen with workmates. On the way home, he pulled off the road near where he had seen the beast to look for any signs it may have left.

"At the time, it freaked me out, so I didn't stop, but it was driving me nuts, what I'd seen," he says. "So I went in there to see if I could find any tracks or something on the ground ... but there was nothing. Just needles from all the birch trees."

Since that day, Tate has tried to find an explanation for the sighting, with little success.

"I've done reading on the Internet, and they talk about bears having mange and how they can get all scrawny and stuff like that, but this thing had a nice, thick coat on it—it didn't look like it had the mange," he says. "It looked healthy. But then with the Bigfoot thing, you always hear that's supposed to be, you know, big. Real big. But this thing was barely over five feet tall."

Though not entirely convinced that what he saw was a Sasquatch-type creature, Tate, a forester, is open to the possibility of Bigfoot as a cryptid living in the vast forests of B.C.

"I've done a bunch of flying over these forests—a lot—and you don't realize till you go up in a plane how much bush is actually out there," he says. "There's so much bush out there that I don't think they've found everything."

Rogers Pass

In addition to reports of missing time and mysterious lights in the sky, Rogers Pass is also home to a growing number of Sasquatch sightings. This phenomenon has been seen on the highway east of Revelstoke since at least sometime prior to the opening of Rogers Pass in 1962.

The first Sasquatch legend comes from the old Big Bend Highway, which connected Revelstoke with Golden prior to the opening of Rogers Pass. According to the story, a couple driving north from Golden collided with a hairy, ape-like creature that walked like a man. The frantic couple pulled the wounded animal off to the side of the road and went for help, but by the time they returned it was gone; the crumpled grill of their car and some blood smears were all that remained.

Cathy English, curator of the Revelstoke Museum and Archives, remembers a man inquiring about local Sasquatch lore at some point in the late 1990s or early 2000s. As there is absolutely no local lore on the subject aside from the aforementioned story, of which she was unaware, English was unable to help the man and he left without leaving a name. What little she recalls of the exchange involved the man telling her that he had encountered something resembling Sasquatch on Highway 1 east of Revelstoke, in Rogers Pass.

Several years later, in 2005, a family traveling west toward Revelstoke was forced to a grinding halt when the semi truck ahead of them stopped suddenly for what appeared to be an enormous, muscled, ape-like creature crossing the highway in front of it. The awestruck family observed the creature as it crossed the road, seemingly disappearing over a precipice on the other side.

The next sighting would be in 2010 when a column of traffic slowed to allow a tall, black, ape-like creature to cross the road; the beast then disappeared up the mountainside. Afterward, one witness turned his vehicle around and searched for signs of the beast along the road and up into the heavy brush but found nothing.

Whatever the true nature of these sightings, they are further proof that the Rogers Pass area holds deeper mysteries than we ever could have imagined.

CHAPTER 32
The Pass

Of all the stories in this book, the one of the Rogers Pass Fireball was the hardest to research because those who actually witnessed the event are reluctant to even acknowledge it happened, let alone talk about it. The bulk of what I know comes from a man who wasn't present but heard about the event soon afterward. The man posted the eyewitness account to a UFO-themed website in the late 1990s/early 2000s and was contacted by a researcher at the University of California who believed what the men witnessed was the testing of an energy weapon, the design of which was based on the work of Serbian inventor Nikola Tesla. The two eyewitnesses I could locate were aware of this theory but disputed it because they believed what they saw was alive. The details in this chapter come from personal interviews with the witnesses.

The two eyewitnesses refused to provide any information as to the identity of the others who were present during the event, but I hope my keeping their confidence will encourage others to come forward.

The story "Missing Time" is adapted from an anonymous account submitted to the website UFO*BC (www. ufobc.ca).

My efforts to identify and locate the person involved, whom I call Henry Talbot, have so far been unsuccessful.

Prior to 1882, the area now known as Rogers Pass, a steep, avalanche-prone passage through the Selkirk Mountains some forty miles east of Revelstoke, was largely unexplored. When, in 1881, the Canadian Pacific Railway decided to run track south through the Rocky Mountains, it became necessary to find a safe route through the treacherous terrain, and Major A.B. Rogers, an American railway location engineer, was chosen for the task. Rogers trekked through that unforgiving country the following year, plotting out a route that, while not risk-free, was the safest possible at the time. Construction on the line began in 1883.

Opening in 1885, the newly christened Rogers Pass immediately became the most dangerous part of Canada's transcontinental railway; between 1883 and 1911, the region's avalanches claimed more than 250 lives. To put that into perspective, since 1782 Canada has recorded a total of 702 avalanche-related fatalities.

The section of the pass between Cheops Mountain and Avalanche Mountain is the infamous site of the deadliest avalanche in Canadian history, and second deadliest in the history of North America—the 1910 Rogers Pass Avalanche, when a frozen section of mountain swept down from Avalanche Peak and buried fifty-eight men under thirty-three feet of snow and ice.

It is also here, in this remote place, where people have encountered some of the most frightening phenomena reported in the Revelstoke area.

"All of a sudden the sky went like daylight"

In the moments leading up to the Rogers Pass Fireball, there was no indication to the few present that this still winter night was different from any other. Temperatures hovered around freezing on the morning of December 18, 1997, as three two-man CPR crews, two aboard trains and one headed home to Revelstoke in a taxi, watched the night sky erupt.

Even some fifteen years later, witnesses to the Rogers Pass Fireball were reluctant to discuss details of the incident. "I haven't talked about it since it happened," says one man who refused to say anything else on the record, "and I don't want to start now."

What details that have emerged tell of a booming sound followed by the appearance of an enormous yellow ball of light, crackling with what appeared to be electricity, streaking across the canyon. Says one source, "All of a sudden the sky went like daylight—bright daylight—and this big yellow ball slowly went over the valley."

The fireball, which made no sound after its initial appearance, was then said to stop its progress and hover above the valley for ten full seconds before finally disappearing behind Mount Sir Donald in the southeast.

While, in the broad strokes, the Revelstoke Fireball shares characteristics with bolides—particularly large and bright meteors entering the earth's atmosphere—these typically disappear in a matter of seconds, whereas the Revelstoke Fireball endured for almost a full minute. Additionally, this is not the first time such a phenomenon has been reported; on March 9, 1957, a Pan Am flight bound from New York for San Juan, Puerto

Rico, narrowly avoided a collision with what was described as a "big fireball advancing with tremendous speed with a roaring sound."

Though reports of the Pan Am encounter do not suggest any kind of intelligence behind the sudden, mysterious conflagration, and other fireballs observed throughout history are often attributed to some as-yet-unknown feature of the natural world, witnesses to the Revelstoke Fireball are almost certain there were more than environmental factors at work.

"I don't know what it was," says another witness who claimed the light was so intense that other drivers on the highway began to swerve in shock. "But I felt like it was looking at us."

Missing Time

Though what follows is the only story of "missing time" to come out of the Revelstoke area, it is far from unique. Missing time episodes are a staple of paranormal lore, usually associated with the field of UFOlogy and cited by true believers as proof of extraterrestrial abduction. While that may seem fantastical, the circumstances surrounding episodes of missing time seem to defy all current understandings of time and space, making it understandable why the first explanation people reach for is literally out of this world.

It begins with silence; while there have been reported instances of group missing time events, it is most common among those who are alone. The person, be they traveling or at home, experiences a momentary disorientation, then observes that a significant amount of time has passed—anywhere from minutes to hours to, in extreme cases, days. Several things differentiate this from simple sleep, the first being that, aside from disorientation and a feeling of "returning"—as though from a general anesthetic—the person experiences no fatigue, dreams, or any other sign of sleep. Second, the episodes often occur while subjects are in motion—driving, walking, etc.—without any loss of motor control. Third, and perhaps most bizarrely, people who have experienced missing time also tend to "wake up" in different places than where their initial disorientation occurred; some people even report waking to find they traveled a far greater distance than should have been possible given the time elapsed during their fugue.

Those who have undergone episodes of lost time are often reluctant to discuss their experience and, while they may not dream during the event, it is extremely common to dream afterward. Often these dreams are not pleasant, as Henry Talbot would discover.

The Nightmare Lights

When he left his Golden, British Columbia, home for Revelstoke on the night of October 5, 2002, Henry Talbot was no stranger to the winding, 150-kilometer section of Highway 1 that connected the two towns via Rogers Pass.

"I had left about 9 p.m., driving alone," he told UFO reporting site *UFO*BC*. "Having driven the route many times—and usually at night—I expected to arrive in Revelstoke before 10:30 p.m."

The danger inherent in traversing Rogers Pass didn't end with the coming of the railroad, even for those accustomed to the trip. Since the highway's completion in 1962, there have been hundreds if not thousands of fatalities on its many curves and bends; one eight-kilometer section just outside of Golden is home to thirty-six curves, including infamous "School Bus

Corner" where, in 1990, a bus crash killed two young girls and injured twenty-eight.

As he set out that fall evening, Talbot knew that despite his familiarity, he would have to be careful on his journey west, and it is this heightened awareness that calls into question more mundane explanations of the following events.

The first twenty to thirty minutes of Talbot's journey were uneventful; the weather had been mild over the last few days and the highway was bare. It is from this point on that events take a strange turn.

"There is a point on the eastern side of Rogers Pass where, if you're heading west, the highway runs straight for a stretch, then takes a sweeping turn to the right," says Talbot. "It then begins to climb toward the summit, passing through snow sheds [concrete tunnels built over highways to deflect avalanches] on the way up."

As he approached the turn, Talbot observed what appeared to be the taillights of a semi truck disappearing around the curve.

"Next thing I know," says Talbot, "I feel like I'm lost. The road seems unfamiliar—level and even a little downhill—not the steep climb to Rogers Pass I was expecting to find around the corner."

Disoriented, Talbot checked his dashboard clock.

"The car clock showed that it's a little before 11 p.m. and that makes me all the more confused. Then I passed a sign that says Revelstoke is only a few kilometers away."

Talbot was then able to place his location but was at a loss to explain how, given the attention he'd been paying the road, he had traveled more than a hundred kilometers without realizing it.

"I do not remember driving through any of the snow sheds on the way up or down," he says. "How could I not remember even one of them? I don't remember driving through Rogers Pass summit, where I'm normally very aware of road and weather conditions, not to mention the bright lights and speed zones."

Initially, Talbot blamed fatigue for the gaps in his memory, but the explanation was an uneasy one.

"I said to myself, 'Who hasn't driven a familiar route and not remembered parts of it?'" he explains. "But still I wondered how I could have forgotten so much—almost the entire trip—and how it was I ended up more than thirty minutes behind schedule."

As he left his Revelstoke hotel the next morning, Talbot found his memory of the previous night's events as hazy as before, but the gaps bothered him less, at least consciously.

"I still felt like something about my trip wasn't right, but it seemed very distant," he says. "For some reason, I also felt as though I would be happier not having to travel that route again."

In the years since that night, Talbot has done his best to abide by that mysterious feeling, taking that particular stretch of Highway 1 only once more, in 2005.

"I traveled that road once more ... with a passenger, at midday, and keeping other traffic in sight at all times," he remembers. "I felt very uneasy on the stretch of road below Rogers Pass."

Though over the years he may have physically returned to Rogers Pass only once, Talbot has found himself mentally returning again and again to that night in 2002.

"I have often had dreams about that trip, the parts of it that I remember," he says. "As if I'm driving it over and over."

One dream in particular has come to haunt him more than any other.

"In one dream, I watch the lights of the semi truck ahead as they began to go around the corner. Suddenly, the lights reverse direction and within a second or so close the distance and fly over my car. I'm leaning forward in the driver seat, craning my neck to look upward through the windshield, where I see a single, large red light a few feet above my car. I'm suddenly filled with terror and ... feel like I can't breathe. I begin hyperventilating and try to cry out for help but only make hoarse squeaking sounds. Then I wake up."

Though he's not convinced that this nightmare is any more than exactly that and he has no concrete explanation for his fear, Henry Talbot still cannot bear the thought of driving Rogers Pass again.

"I do not want to be on that road," he says, "and I don't really understand why."

CHAPTER 33

Whispers

After three years of interviewing people in the Revelstoke area, I realized experiences like those in this book are practically commonplace, but because of lingering social stigmas surrounding the paranormal, many people choose to keep their stories to themselves. I lost count of how many people chose not to talk because they were afraid friends and neighbors would think less of them for it. What this means is that for every account you have read in this book, there is likely another that has, for one reason or another, gone untold. Thanks again to Brian Vike for allowing me access to his archive of UFO sighting reports.

In some cases, whispers of a story have made their way to me but have been so slight as to be impossible to develop further, the involved parties have declined to speak on the record, or there are simply no living witnesses. Here, we record some of those whispers so that the stories are not lost entirely. The stories below are broken into two types: UFO-style encounters, and experiences that suggest contact with the realm of the dead and other planes of existence outside our town.

Strange Skies

Elsewhere in this book, I say that I don't believe UFOs are extraterrestrial beings come to earth in physical craft, and that's about all I "know" on the subject. John Keel's ultraterrestrial theory is compelling, as is a remark made by remote viewer Joe McMoneagle at a meeting of the Mutual UFO Network (MUFON) Los Angeles. McMoneagle described remote viewing a UFO incident and feeling as though, rather than a physical craft, the phenomenon was like two tin cans on a string, with the UFO as one can and the other being in some higher dimension. Whatever the case, since 1950 there have been countless UFO sightings in the skies around Revelstoke, and though not all of them are dramatic enough to warrant an entire chapter of their own, each story is a piece of a much larger puzzle:

In the mid-1950s, a young boy and his father spied, at midday, a large, metallic, cigar-shaped object in the air ten or twenty feet above a gas station and general store in the part of town known as Big Eddy. The pair observed the object for several minutes until it rose out of sight.

Sometime in the mid-1950s, a woman living in the now-drowned Arrow Lakes community of Sidmouth was hanging her washing when a silver disc passed not far overhead, traveling at great speed. A man re-shingling his roof also happened to see the object.

The most dramatic alleged UFO case in Revelstoke's history, included here for completion's sake only, comes from a night in 1963 or 1964, when a woman claims that the light and noise from an unidentified craft emptied out bars and restaurants as people flooded the streets to see it. According to the witness, the craft "had what appeared to be an outer casing that revolved around the body with circular cut-outs. As it passed over the red areas, a light appeared to blink but in reality never shut off." While the event may have happened as described, not a single person I spoke to who lived in Revelstoke around that time remembers any such event and, if such a thing did happen, it didn't rate a mention in the local newspapers for either of those years.

During the winter of 1970, a silver disc-shaped object was seen above town before disappearing over the horizon.

Just after midnight on December 5, 1979, a police officer in the town of Kamloops, 220 kilometers west of Revelstoke, sighted an orange light, similar to a flare, which disappeared within seconds. Shortly thereafter, the officer was shocked by the appearance of a thousand-foot-long object, its arrival heralded by a blast from its six or eight bright white lights. The object remained stationary, between one-fourth and one-half mile off the ground, for ten to fifteen seconds before soundlessly rocketing off to the east, where it disappeared from sight. Authorities in Revelstoke sighted it twenty minutes later. The official explanation was that a Russian spaceship had re-entered the atmosphere but other such events have been seen elsewhere in the years since, with no explanation offered.

Also in the Big Eddy, this time in the 1990s, two men working on a campground observed, in broad daylight, what looked like three bullets flashing across Mount Begbie. The men say the objects moved too quickly and too silently to be jets.

A prominent member of a local church reportedly saw so many UFOs in the skies above Revelstoke he stopped keeping track of them. The deeply devout Christian was deeply troubled by the sightings, which he believed to be manifestations of Satan.

Around 1 a.m. sometime on a morning in the 1990s, two teenagers who had been sitting in their backyard drinking spotted a reddish light in the sky above. Described as looking almost like a shooting star, the light shot from east to west, before changing direction above Mount Begbie and disappearing over the horizon to the south. The shaken teens spent the rest of the night inside.

In May 2000, a man coming home from work spotted two rotating lines of multicolored lights, roughly one meter apart and four meters in diameter, hovering above the train tracks on Victoria Avenue. The lights followed the train tracks away to the east, faster than the man could run, and swiftly disappeared from sight.

In the early 2000s, a man claims to have seen the moon take the shape of a woman's face. He says the effect lasted for some thirty seconds before being obscured by clouds.

In 2001, while in the Arrow Lakes region, a man observed a bright white light, similar to an aircraft landing light, slowly descend on a mountain before disappearing. The impact, if that's what it was, produced no explosion, fire, or smoke.

In May 2006, a man observed, at roughly 2 a.m., a series of lights in a boomerang shape flying back and forth below the clouds. The object, which also had two lights at the back, made three or four passes as it ascended, eventually disappearing into the clouds.

Early evening, December 2007: A mother and daughter sitting in their vehicle saw a flat, oval object with five or six flashing lights in the center. The pair watched the light for five to ten seconds before it disappeared behind the treeline.

While looking at vacation photographs taken in Rogers Pass during a Vancouver-to-Calgary drive, a family noticed what appeared to be a curved, light-emitting flying vehicle following them in three sequential photos. The object was not visible at the time the photographs were taken.

In 2009, a father and son observed what they first thought was a helicopter hovering fifty feet above the tree line. Upon inspection, they realized the "helicopter" was not disturbing the trees below it, had greenish lights, and had a kind of fog around it. Only a few moments after they saw the object, it fled at a speed far faster than that of any helicopter.

In November 2009 a couple living near 3 Valley Gap, twenty-three kilometers west of Revelstoke on Highway 1, saw a spherical light moving in the sky, beginning around 1 a.m. and lasting for roughly thirty minutes. The light looked like a firework when it first appeared but stayed in the sky, sometimes moving erratically. It split into two lights, which moved independently of one another before uniting again and disappearing.

Around 8:45 p.m. on September 2, 3, and 4, 2010, a couple living near Trout Lake, fifty kilometers west of Revelstoke, spotted a round white light moving slowly across the sky. It was described as moving slower than a satellite but made no noise and did not have a plane's blinking light.

In February 2015, someone captured on video a triangular-shaped object—black on top with blue lights on the bottom—in the night sky.

One night in April 2015, a young woman noticed what look like a procession of stars—five points of light in a vertical line—

moving from west to east across the sky. Having first observed them in the vicinity of Venus to the northwest, the lights—described as being all white and of varying brightness—moved slowly and soundlessly before simply disappearing.

Spirit and the World around Us

There is no question more pertinent to the human experience than that of life after death. Do we really pass from the physical realm after life ends, and if so, where do we go? Furthermore, if there are dimensions beyond the physical, what is their nature and are they home to beings other than ourselves? Below are brief stories that suggest there are more things in heaven and earth than are, well, you know the drill:

Revelstoke's now-demolished second hospital, the Queen Victoria Cottage Hospital, was said to be haunted. A woman who worked there during its final years remembers another nurse returning to her station screaming she had seen an apparition—the torso of a female—gliding through the air on the third floor.

A night janitor working at Cooper's Foods, a supermarket built on part of the former hospital site, reportedly quit his job because a spirit was tormenting him at work. The janitor, a man in his mid-fifties by all accounts struggling with drug addiction, would often see the figure of a woman in the store's bakery section. One night he noticed a drawer ajar, and when he pushed it back in, another, adjacent drawer popped open. He closed that, only to have another do the same. This went on for a few minutes until the last drawer closed and he looked up to see a disembodied face staring back at him. The specter disappeared almost immediately.

The now-shuttered ABC Country Restaurant, which was once adjacent to Cooper's Foods, was also said to be a hub of activity. A former manager tells of a strange whistling sound in the back of the building, which she is certain was not caused by airflow and would disappear whenever she or anyone else approached. There are also reports of visiting dogs barking at thin air in the back office.

In the 1960s, a young boy was downstairs in the basement of his family's Eighth Street home when he heard a rustling in the next room. Assuming it was his mother, the boy called out a greeting, which was met by a soft laugh and more rustling. The boy ran upstairs, where he found his mother sitting at the table with a cup of coffee. He didn't leave her side the rest of the day.

Workers and residents at a local seniors' housing complex have reported feeling a crushing sense of dread in the days prior to the unexpected deaths of residents. This is most commonly felt in the communal eating area, often at night but sometimes during the day as well. In the basement of this same complex, some people have reported mobile cold spots and a heavy sense of presence, though this has no apparent ties to resident deaths. I have experienced these cold spots, which seem to produce a creeping sense of paralysis the closer to them you get.

Following the death of a local man in the mid-2000s, his family, who were spread throughout British Columbia and Alberta, began to simultaneously see and interact with butterflies; sometimes one lone butterfly would be sitting in an unlikely place, sometimes huge clouds would appear and disappear in a matter of seconds. Each member of the family was unaware of each other's experiences until months after the fact.

While walking through the graveyard at dusk, a woman watched what looked like a female apparition running roughly three feet above the ground. The specter crossed several rows of tombstones before simply disappearing.

A seemingly innocuous basement storage room in a Taylor Street home always held a heavy feeling of dread for the young man who lived there. Though it often spread into the whole basement—to the point where he disliked locking the door in case he needed to make a speedy exit—the small storage room was always the most frightening spot.

Though many people speak about haunting in Minto Manor, an imposing neoclassical heritage home and B&B on McKenzie Avenue, there have been few reported cases of unusual activity, most of which revolve around a mysterious cold spot on the first floor. In one particular instance, on a hot summer day, a guide from the local tourism office walked into what she described as "a cold column of air" in the main parlor. The young woman ran from the building and never went back. On another occasion, a man of Maori descent visiting from New Zealand claimed to have had a sleepless night because of what felt like intense scrutiny by an unseen observer. A handful of other guests have also reported feeling the presence of a small dog, though the current owner of Minto Manor has not had any pets while living in the house.

Not far away, in another house on McKenzie Avenue, a shrouded woman is said to sometimes watch passersby from an attic window. The home was once a part of the local tourist office's haunted house tour, which has been discontinued for several years.

In yet another house on that section of McKenzie, a family would often, at all hours of the day, see shadows flitting at the edge of their vision and, on rare occasions, full humanoid figures sliding down hallway walls. Also common were mysterious banging noises from upstairs.

In April 2013, it was just after eight in the evening when a young woman stepped out onto her front porch for a cigarette. Before she could light the cigarette, she saw her stepfather sitting in the front seat of his truck, which was parked at the curb thirty feet away. She froze; the man had been dead for a month. The man turned to look at her, and then vanished. Several nights later, the young woman had a waking dream in which she saw, from her bed, a shadowy figure approach her daughter's room. She tried to protest but found herself unable to move. The unidentifiable figure, however, immediately appeared at her bedside and said, "It's okay. It's not what you think." She fell asleep soon after. In the morning, her five-year-old daughter told her how Grandpa had come to her in her dreams. The child said the two "washed dishes, laughed, and played hopscotch." The young woman never dreamed of the figure again.

A girl dressed all in white is sometimes seen walking down the middle of Victoria Road near the Railway Museum. Most often seen between 7 p.m. and midnight, she is said to give off a positive feeling.

The pedestrian bridge off the Greenbelt is said to be home to another positive spirit, though no one can say for certain what it looks like.

In the early morning hours, a couple living in a house they purchased from the estate of a deceased Italian couple sometimes see two grainy humanoid figures watching them. On one occasion, a troublesome houseguest who would not leave was shoved so hard into a wall by an unseen force that her arm was broken. Some nights when the homeowners fall asleep downstairs in the living room, they are awakened around 3 a.m. by a voice that sharply says, "Go upstairs!"

A family, none of whom were smokers, would sometimes smell cigarette smoke in their home. Finally, one day their eldest daughter saw a tall, thin man wearing a fisherman's cap smoking in the upstairs hallway. He disappeared almost immediately. He would reappear on occasion, sometimes wearing the hat and sometimes not.

In the 1950s, a boy and his family were visiting town to attend the funeral of a favorite uncle. The house where his uncle had lived was filled with mourners, and so the boy ended up having to sleep in his uncle's former bed. When he awoke the next morning, a small metal St. Christopher's medallion had been placed on his chest. When he brought the medallion downstairs to show his family, not one of them knew where it had come from.

A woman was asleep in bed one night when she was jolted awake just in time to see her grandfather approach. The elderly man bent at the waist to have a look at the prone woman, smiled, then stood and disappeared. The man had been dead for several decades.

For months after the death of her mother, a woman would hear the back door of her house opening and closing at 1 p.m., the same time of day her mother used to come over for coffee. This would happen whether or not the door was bolted shut.

Some former residents of the apartment building known as the Pink Castle would hear footsteps in the upstairs apartment, followed by what sounded like heavy furniture being dragged across the floor. This would only happen when the upstairs apartment was empty.

Former residents of a small house near the corner of Second and Robson Street remember hearing the sound of footsteps when everyone had gone to bed. This occurred during their childhood and again years later when they visited the home.

A reporter who had conducted interviews in Holten House for a story on the property went back to review his recordings and found them mysteriously corrupted. Recordings on the same tape made in other locations were still listenable.

Employees at a small grocery store would sometimes see a shadowy human figure watching them from the corners of the room. On certain nights, one particular employee would feel as though someone was following him home at the end of his shift, and on those nights his sleep was plagued by terrible nightmares.

The teenage son of a family living on First Street began to have run-ins with what they believed was an "earth spirit," an energy being that is neither human nor animal. The conflict went on for months until a friend of the family suggested burying a copper talisman on either side of the home, which he believed would disrupt the spirit's ability to enter. The spirit never returned.

When they were filling coolers or cleaning windows, workers at the Skyline Truck Stop on Highway 1 would often see the reflection of a strange man standing behind them, but he would be gone by the time they turned around. When the truck stop burned down on November 2, 2015, the man had not been seen in a number of years.

The Hartland Diner, now a Denny's, was said to be haunted by a spirit who would move kitchen items around in the night.

Frying pans would often go missing, only to turn up again days later.

The residents of a Fourth Street home have one bedroom they call "the dream room" because anyone who sleeps in that room experiences vivid dreams. No other room in the house has the same effect.

One day Dan Marsh, an employee of the Revelstoke Dam, was working alone in an electrical room when he was passed by a co-worker. The two men greeted one another, the co-worker passed into a neighboring room, and Marsh kept on with his work until several minutes later when he realized that not only was the man totally unknown to him but the safety gear he had been wearing was years out of date. Intending to question the man, Marsh went into the room where he had gone, but the co-worker was nowhere to be found. He had not passed Marsh again on the way out and the room had no other exits; it was as if the man had simply disappeared.

A man living in a famously haunted house near the courthouse took to calling the spirit in his home Harold and would chastise the ghost for making trouble. The spirit liked to mess with his television's reception, to which the man would say, "Okay, Harold, stop it!" After he said this, the reception would, unfailingly, correct itself.

Roger Ayles, former owner of the now-closed Video Express, used to joke with his staff that, should he ever die, he would find a way to haunt them. Weeks after the man's sudden passing in 2010, the video box for horror film *A Nightmare on Elm Street* started turning up in odd locations throughout the store. No matter how many times staff replaced the box, it would have been moved somewhere else by morning. This lasted for several weeks.

One family believes their resident ghost would sometimes follow guests home, as strange happenings—items moving from one place to another, strange noises—would stop in one location and begin in another. When this happened, the family would go to the house where the spirit had set up residence, open the car door and tell the invisible force it was time to go home. The phenomena would then start back up in their own home.

Conclusion

People often ask why Revelstoke is such a strange little place, whether there's something about the city and surrounding geography that makes it such a lightning rod for the unusual, and the simple answer is: I don't know. Maybe there's a wholly rational explanation for everything—maybe certain concentrations of minerals in the soil attract a particular kind of electrical energy, maybe the magnetic stress produced by fault lines plays havoc with the human brain, or maybe, as one person has suggested to me, radon off-gassing from the land is giving us all some wicked hallucinations. Hell, maybe the movie *Hotel Transylvania* was on to something and ghosts, aliens, and Bigfoot all just really dig vacationing in the mountains. Or, finally, and this is the one I both tend to believe and struggle to accept, Revelstoke sits in a place where the worlds of the living, dead, and things wholly unimaginable overlap in such a way as to allow passage between them.

Some subjects only make sense at night; when the campfire has died to embers and the world around us has gone to sleep, it's much easier to entertain the idea that somewhere out there the barrier between realities has worn thin and through the gap flow creations both wonderful and terrible. As I write this, it's a sunny summer morning, the coffee shop near my apartment where I'm working is full of people—government workers on their coffee breaks and stay-at-home mothers taking a breather from their responsibilities, among others—and the idea of intersecting realities is hard to take seriously. So much of the modern world is built on scientifically proven concepts, things either immediately visible or that we can somehow otherwise quantify, that there doesn't seem to be room for anything else—after all, a moody hipster made my coffee, not a shadow man, and that's not a gremlin crossing the street in those unfortunate zebra-stripe tights.

Yet in recent years the scientific community has advanced theories about the universe—the holographic universe theory and multiverse theory, to name two—which suggest there's a lot more going on around us than we ever could have imagined. When considering the possibility of infinite universes, it suddenly doesn't seem impossible that one or two may be given over to shadows, the dead, and everything else we like to pretend we're too smart to see.

Or that at some nexus point between them all sits Revelstoke, a strange little place with roots in both their worlds and ours.

To Write to the Author

If you wish to contact the author or would like more information about this book, please write to the author in care of Llewellyn Worldwide Ltd. and we will forward your request. Both the author and publisher appreciate hearing from you and learning of your enjoyment of this book and how it has helped you. Llewellyn Worldwide Ltd. cannot guarantee that every letter written to the author can be answered, but all will be forwarded. Please write to:

Brennan Storr
℅ Llewellyn Worldwide
2143 Wooddale Drive
Woodbury, MN 55125-2989

Please enclose a self-addressed stamped envelope for reply,
or $1.00 to cover costs. If outside the U.S.A., enclose
an international postal reply coupon.

Many of Llewellyn's authors have websites with additional information and resources. For more information, please visit our website at http://www.llewellyn.com

GET MORE AT LLEWELLYN.COM

Visit us online to browse hundreds of our books and decks, plus sign up to receive our e-newsletters and exclusive online offers.

- • **Free tarot readings** • **Spell-a-Day** • **Moon phases**
- • **Recipes, spells, and tips** • **Blogs** • **Encyclopedia**
- • **Author interviews, articles, and upcoming events**

GET SOCIAL WITH LLEWELLYN

Find us on

Facebook

www.Facebook.com/LlewellynBooks

Follow us on

twitter

www.Twitter.com/Llewellynbooks

GET BOOKS AT LLEWELLYN

LLEWELLYN ORDERING INFORMATION

Order online: Visit our website at www.llewellyn.com to select your books and place an order on our secure server.

Order by phone:
- • Call toll free within the U.S. at 1-877-NEW-WRLD (1-877-639-9753)
- • Call toll free within Canada at 1-866-NEW-WRLD (1-866-639-9753)
- • We accept VISA, MasterCard, American Express and Discover

Order by mail:
Send the full price of your order (MN residents add 6.875% sales tax) in U.S. funds, plus postage and handling to: Llewellyn Worldwide, 2143 Wooddale Drive Woodbury, MN 55125-2989

POSTAGE AND HANDLING

STANDARD (U.S. & Canada):
(Please allow 12 business days)
$30.00 and under, add $4.00.
$30.01 and over, FREE SHIPPING.

INTERNATIONAL ORDERS:
$16.00 for one book, plus $3.00 for each additional book.

Visit us online for more shipping options.
Prices subject to change.

FREE CATALOG!

To order, call
1-877-
NEW-WRLD
ext. 8236
or visit our
website

THE
GHOSTS
OF
CHICAGO

The Windy City's Most Famous Haunts

ADAM SELZER

The Ghosts of Chicago
The Windy City's Most Famous Haunts
ADAM SELZER

From Resurrection Mary and Al Capone to the Murder Castle of H. H. Holmes and the funeral train of Abraham Lincoln, the spine-tingling sights and sounds of Chicago's yesteryear are still with us... and so are its ghosts.

Seeking to find out what we really know about the ghastly past of this famously haunted metropolis, professional ghost hunter and historian Adam Selzer pieces together the truth behind Chicago's ghosts, and brings to light never-before-told first accounts. Take a history tour like no other of the famous and not-so-famous haunts around town. Sometimes the real story is far different from the urban legend—and most of the time it's even gorier.

978-0-7387-3611-2, 360 pp., 5 ³⁄₁₆ x 8   **$15.99**

RICHARD SOUTHALL

HAUNTED
PLANTATIONS
OF THE
SOUTH

Haunted Plantations of the South
RICHARD SOUTHALL

Step into the mysterious world of haunted plantations, where you'll meet the restless spirits of soldiers, slaves, and owners who roam the antiquated halls. Presenting majestic homes from seven southern states, this remarkable guide contains dramatic history and true stories from the days before and during the Civil War.

Join paranormal expert Richard Southall on an awe-inspiring journey through each plantation, exploring grand houses and their ghastly ghouls. *Haunted Plantations of the South* presents fascinating research, in-depth interviews with ghost hunters, and unforgettable encounters full of paranormal activity and evidence. Discover the phantom casket of the Sweetwater Plantation, the Man in Black who haunts Bellamy Mansion, and many more compelling ghost stories along the way.

978-0-7387-4024-9, 216 pp., 6 x 9 **$15.99**

GHOSTLY TALES OF MUSICAL LEGENDS

HAUNTED
ROCK &
ROLL

MATTHEW L. SWAYNE

Haunted Rock & Roll
Ghostly Tales of Musical Legends
Matthew L. Swayne

From rock and roll's pioneers to its contemporary rebels, explore how the greatest names live on after death—in unexpected and frightening ways. Combining two of America's great passions, celebrities and the paranormal, *Haunted Rock & Roll* covers rock's entire supernatural history.

Explore rock and roll's most iconic idols, haunted locations, and infamous legends through evidence and testimonials from renowned ghost hunters and researchers. Discover thrilling stories of Michael Jackson, Jim Morrison, Led Zeppelin, the Beatles, Amy Winehouse, and many more stars seen haunting their favorite bars, clubs, and homes. From the early days through the present pop music era, rockers have followed the same motto: Live fast, die young, and leave a restless spirit.

978-0-7387-3923-6, 288 pp, 5³⁄₁₆ x 8   **$15.99**

JAMIE DAVIS
WITH SAMUEL QUEEN

INSIDE ABANDONED
INSTITUTIONS
FOR THE CRAZY,
CRIMINAL & QUARANTINED

HAUNTED
ASYLUMS, PRISONS,
AND
SANATORIUMS

Haunted Asylums, Prisons, and Sanatoriums
Inside Abandoned Institutions for the Crazy,
Criminal & Quarantined
JAMIE DAVIS

A chill runs through the air inside the Death Tunnel at Waverly Hills Hospital. The Shadow Man haunts cellblocks at the West Virginia Penitentiary. A Civil War soldier's ghost communicates through flashlights at the Trans-Allegheny Lunatic Asylum. Explore dozens of chilling ghost stories like these and 57 terrifying photographs from ten well-known, haunted institutions across the United States.

Haunted Asylums, Prisons, and Sanatoriums includes the history of each building, personal paranormal experiences from the author and facility staff, and spooky highlights from on-site tours. This spine-tingling, one-of-a-kind guide is filled with photos, historical knowledge, interviews, and frightening, first-hand stories. Readers will also enjoy an introduction to basic ghost hunting equipment and detailed information about organizing their own visits to these haunted institutions.

978-0-7387-3750-8, 240 pp., 6 x 9　　　　　　　　　　**$15.99**
